Books
about
Books

BY WINSLOW L. WEBBER

A Bio-bibliography for Collectors

HALE, CUSHMAN & FLINT
Boston 1937

Republished by Gale Research Company, Book Tower, Detroit, 1974

Library of Congress Cataloging in Publication Data

Webber, Winslow Lewis, 1898-
　Books about books.

　　1. Bibliography--Bibliography.　2. Book collecting--
Bibliography.　I. Title.
Z1002.W37　　1974　　　　016.020'75　　　　73-18456
ISBN 0-8103-3690-1

DEDICATED
TO
E. B. W. IN APPRECIATION
OF HER ENCOURAGEMENT AND
HELPFUL SUGGESTIONS.

PREFACE

It is the writer's hope that this attempt at a contribution to the literature of book collecting will provide a practical tool for the bookman's use. Its failings are acknowledged. It is far from complete yet at least the attempt has been made. Quite probably the criticism and corrections that are bound to follow the publication of a work of this character will serve their purpose in the preparation of an enlarged and corrected volume.

WINSLOW L. WEBBER

Wellesley Hills,
Massachusetts
July 19, 1937

"The true University of these days is a Collection of Books."
THOMAS CARLYLE

TABLE OF Contents

Chapter One

BOOK COLLECTING AND BOOKS ABOUT BOOKS

Page 1-15

Chapter Two

BIO-BIBLIOGRAPHY: THE TEXT BOOKS OF THE COLLECTOR

Page 16-135

Chapter Three

MAGAZINE REFERENCE: A BIBLIOGRAPHY 1900-37

Page 136-162

Glossary

Page 163-168

CHAPTER I

Book Collecting and Books about Books

OF the value of a hobby for the business man little need be said. Not only the physician but others fully as wise to the folly of too close and long continued application to one kind of work have advocated, for the man who would last to live out a full, well rounded life, a change and relaxation at times from the labor by which he earns his daily bread. The wisdom of this advice has been recognized and as a result we have that *genus homo*, the collector. One collects furniture, another, fine glass or English Sporting Prints, but the greatest maniac of all collects books. For most of the sins of man, forgiveness is forthcoming sooner or later, but for the poor book collector there is no reforming or hope and very little of that peace and quiet for which his soul longs. Every time he spends a dollar for a book, his wife spends two or more for an oil lamp without a wick, or something equally valueless, at least in the eyes of the collector, and nags him into the bargain with the repeated question, "What good are your old books, anyway?"

Woe unto him, for the book collector himself admits he is crazy or, to put it another way, he is sane enough to recognize his eccentricities. His business associates who listen with respect to the ideas he may advance for making one dollar grow into two, lapse into a painful and hurt silence when he suggests that the same or, in fact, even larger percentage of profit is possible in the market for rare books. They feel in their hearts that undoubtedly something is the matter with this otherwise seemingly healthy associate, and right they are for he is afflicted with a most incurable and insidious disease long known among collectors and dealers as bibliomania.

One suffering from bibliomania is known as a bibliomaniac, and among mortals there is no human comparison unless one considers the statistician who, in his own field of research, if current comment is to be believed, is as wild as any book collector. However, when the statistician's compilation of data is added, the result is simply another series of digits, but the collector in adding

BOOKS ABOUT BOOKS

up his efforts finds himself possessed of a source of fascination to which he can safely retire and which in turn will give him everything that is best in life. Books sum up all the thoughts, imagination and discoveries that man has made. By their help and influence one acquires resources and pleasures that nothing else can give. What is more important, the collecting of books offers a refuge which enables the bibliophile to come into possession of thoughts which put to rout not only many ills of the body, but the worries as well with which today most men are still sorely beset.

The books that a man buys and keeps are more indicative of his character than the size of his bank account or the people with whom he associates. Books remain after a man's lifetime as mute reminders of the extent of his emotions and the degree of his intellect. Men have an abiding faith in books which, unlike human associates, do not disappoint them. The comforting and eternal solace of a book is more to be desired than the changing words of men which unfortunately cannot be trusted or relied upon as can the printed page. Throughout their relatively short period of existence books have become part and parcel of man. They will live and be sought for long after their original creators or owners have passed away.

According to the ENCYCLOPEDIA BRITANNICA, a definition of book collecting is "the assembling of books which in their individual and associate form seem to have some element of permanent value and of which the known copies are limited in number." Actually, it is difficult to forecast either the author or the particular category of books that will have permanent value. Furthermore, for one to restrict collecting activities solely to books of known, limited numbers would greatly reduce the number of collectors and their activities. Consequently, while the writer has no desire to take issue with the ENCYCLOPEDIA BRITANNICA on any definition, it would seem more fitting to include in a definition of book collecting the systematic and regular acquisition of the books of any author or any subject, regardless of their known scarcity, present or future value.

It seems safe from contradiction to refer to book collecting as a science, for certainly if one is to become a true as well as successful collector, exact knowledge is essential. Webster's dictionary defines science as "any branch or department of systematized knowledge" and again, "knowledge as of principles or facts." Certainly in the collecting of books, as in the pursuit of no other hobby, one must be sure of his facts as represented by the various "points" of the editions with which he is concerned.

BOOK COLLECTING AND BOOKS ABOUT BOOKS

It is essential that the collecting of books come within the bounds of an exact science. Knowledge of facts is as fundamental in book collecting as in mathematics. In both instances, one is either right or wrong. Far too many errors have been committed already under the guise of bibliography to permit of many more, but one can hardly be expected to confine his collecting endeavors to such rules as may be proposed by any who have a selfish interest in seeing the popular trend of collecting sway from one subject or one author to another. Of course, fashions have always existed in book collecting and always will. In one year the journals and catalogues will be filled with praise of Eighteenth Century Literature; at another time, in earnest exhortation of Modern Authors or the Elizabethan Dramatists. It is earnestly hoped that the embryo collector will not attempt to follow the fashions in the game or what for the moment seems the most popular subject or author, but rather that he will follow the dictates of his own heart. Most of all, the collector must read the books that he buys, although there are many who will take exception to this statement. This last he is bound to do if he remains indifferent to the popular trend. In the end, if he sticks to his own pre-conceived plan, he will have a library of value to others as well as to himself, and at the same time he will know the comforting sensation of having assembled and, in effect, created a collection of books that quite possibly is not duplicated. Such a library is bound to be unique if it bears evidence of the owner's personality as reflected in his taste and judgment. The sincere collector who is honest with himself, therefore, will not be distracted by any expression of popular fancy. He will continue on his own sweet way and as the months and years go on, he will be amazed at the extent to which his collection has grown and the value it has acquired.

While there are records of the activities of book collectors from the time of Petrach (1304-1374), who was a forerunner of Aldus Manutius in the origin and evolution of books, it is rather surprising that there is such a scarcity of literature regarding a subject which has so completely held the interests of men throughout past centuries down to the present time. One astonishing characteristic of book collecting is its steady cumulative growth. Regardless of war, plague, economic change or the most disastrous events that history chronicles, the love of men for books and the acquisitive instinct that impels them to buy and preserve books and to pass them on to those who follow after is an outstanding redeeming factor in a world that has suffered much since its creation. The perennial interest of men in books has probably done more than religion

BOOKS ABOUT BOOKS

or any other present or inherited grace to excuse the civilization of our predecessors.

Nations war against one another; a conquering emperor proclaims that all books must be destroyed lest they put strange thoughts into the minds of his latest subjects and thus endanger his new throne. His edict becomes law, but back in the Middle Ages we have glimpses of monks, the only learned men of their time, feverishly walling up in some remote part of their subterranean cloisters what small portion of their slim stock of books they can hide before soldiers put into effect the king's word.

Manuscripts and books, more than any other material items, have been preserved throughout the years. As a library to an educational institution, so often is a single book the very soul and existence of a collector. Neither family threats nor even lack of funds can curb the desire to add just one more volume to his collection. Never was there a more insidious disease than this bibliomania, as Dibdin, in the eighteenth century, so aptly named the craze for book collecting. And how under its spell do collections grow! No contraceptive has ever successfully retarded the collecting of books. Collectors have literally been forced out of house and home by the growth of their libraries. History records at least one collector whose walls, floor and bed itself, piled high with books, succumbed from the very weight of their presence: It is significant to note, however, that though the man died, his books remained.

Astonishingly few books are destroyed by natural causes, by fire, for example. Singly or in mass, books are about as difficult objects to destroy by burning as any combustible objects owing to the exclusion of the necessary oxygen through their tightly sewed and bound pages. While in his interesting little monograph called THE ENEMIES OF BOOKS, published in London in 1888, Blades claims that, of the ten destroyers of books, "not one has been half so destructive as fire," in modern history there has not been any serious loss of important collections by fire, except the direct cause be war, as when the magnificant Library of Strasbourg was burned by the shells of the German Army in 1870 and again in the World War during the invasion of French territory by the Germans, when the contents of the Louvain Library were similarly destroyed.

Countless books have come down to us from the past, and because their heirs have appreciated them as legacies, they have survived not only their previous owners but in a majority of instances the brick, wood, mortar and stone

BOOK COLLECTING AND BOOKS ABOUT BOOKS

which at one time or another gave them shelter. A good example is the collapse, a few years ago, of the walls of the Vatican Library in Rome. Many books are fragile in their construction and would not only soil easily but gradually disintegrate from careless handling. Fortunately, in their very weakness lies their strength, for what men cherish they handle carefully.

There is no short cut to the successful acquisition of a collection of books. Considerable patience in waiting for certain items to show up in some dealer's catalogue or at an auction must be exercised as the hunt continues for the particular books needed to strengthen a special collection. Each new purchase, provided it falls within the vacant place on the shelf in its proper order and is not simply the result of haphazard buying, will give to the collector the happiness that comes from knowing that one more essential unit has been added to the library he is carefully assembling.

This thought is, of course, based upon the assumption that a collector to be worthy of the name must be seriously interested in one or more authors or the literature of some particular subject rather than in simply acquiring a conglomerate lot of unrelated books. Unfortunately, a vast number of errors can be concealed by one who is a collector, for example, of a subject as broad as that of Americana. Only the late Henry E. Huntington with his vast collections, now permanently housed at San Marino, California and purchased on a wholesale basis without thought or regard for price, might qualify as a real collector of Americana. Perhaps that statement should be modified, for Huntington was a buyer rather than a collector. The very extent of his purchases precluded him from ever experiencing the joys of the average collector who must make some financial sacrifice if he is to continue his modest purchases. One has only to glance through the bibliographies and catalogues of Americana to realize the impossible task of assembling a library of which the owner might be said even to approach the dignity of being classified as a collector within this field. The most that a careful collector can hope to accomplish in a lifetime and without the expenditure of a fortune is to confine himself to a single branch of this broad subject.

Sabastian Brant in his SHYP OF FOLYS sought to ridicule the prevailing follies and vices of every rank and profession under the allegory of a ship freighted with fools. He did not neglect the book collector, and Alexander Barclay in his translation printed in Black Letter by Pymson of London in 1509 has drawn only too clearly in the following lines the character of the collector who, to the dealer's joy but to the bibliomaniac's regret, possesses large funds but little taste:

> "Styll and I besy bokes assemblynage,
> For to have plenty it is a pleasant thynge
> In my conceyt, and to have them ay in honde:
> But what they mene do I not understande."

Even in ignorance, however, the wealthy collector of books on a large scale performs a valuable service in the amassing of huge stores of books. The small collector may decry the unlimited bid by which the agent of the collector of means is able to secure at auction the prize items of the lot. He knows full well that, given the power that money would provide, he, too, would force prices up to the point where competition must necessarily stop. After all, some credit is due the man of wealth, or perhaps more properly the dealer who first drew his attention to books, for the valuable collections that he brings together and which he invariably, particularly in this country, eventually makes accessible to the properly accredited student and often to the public at large. The student and less fortunate collector must frequently overlook a lack of bibliographical knowledge in admiration and recognition of the vast scale upon which, through his various agents often scattered throughout the world, the rich man creates his library. Without doubt he employs the same fundamental executive principles of organization, strategy and understanding of human nature which enabled him to amass his fortune.

Henry E. Huntington, who died in 1927, is a perfect example of this type of collector. His expenditures for books made him the foremost buyer at auctions that ever lived. His recorded purchases at the Hoe, Church, Britwell Court and Bridgewater Library sales totaled $3,050,000 and his books from other sources cost fully as much in addition.

All collectors cannot be Huntingtons and fully as much credit for the preservation of books is due the man of limited means who within his small field is an earnest and sincere collector. Many books which might otherwise have perished from neglect or never have become known have been sought out, protected and saved for posterity by collectors whose names are unknown. Furthermore, far more notable from the point of view of his personal credit, and his contribution to literature and as an example to others is the act of the collector who concentrates upon some unknown but to him interesting author or who gathers such books as he can on any one particular subject. Such effort, however remote from popular interest or demand, may come to have considerable research value to the student. It is by no means forever lost, and one who has such an interest at heart may truly be classed as a collector.

In the midst of the present hectic scramble for a living in which, with varying degrees of success, the majority of us are engaged, it is restful to the bookman to contemplate the acquisition of books and the existence of libraries. No lover of books can cross the threshold of a great library, be it private or public, without being filled with a spirit of reverence. He can but salute the founder of the place and ponder upon the fact that, as the books gathered there have already outlived their many previous owners, so they will outlive by many days and years the destructible clay of his own miserable body. A truer statement with respect to books, quoted again from Sebastian Brant, has yet to be written:

>"For out of olde feldes, as men seith
>Cometh al this new corn fro yeer to yere;
>And out of olde bokes, in good feith,
>Cometh al this new science that men lere."

A book, let it be understood, to a growing number of individuals the world over quite transcends material substance. It possesses to the initiated a mysterious ethereal quality. No longer is it a question as to whether or not the literary treasures of any day or age produce feelings of veneration on the part of those who seek them out and come in contact with them. The great increase in modern times in the number of active collectors large and small together with the growth of public and private libraries is witness to the influence of books upon men.

Unfortunately for the dealer as well as for the peace of mind of the collector himself, there are still countless practically minded individuals who can find no merit in book collecting aside from its function of putting into circulation relatively large sums of money. Such individuals see only the wisdom of buying today to sell at a profit tomorrow. Such gambling in books is distasteful to the true collector. Lacking as they do any generous understanding or moral support on the part of the public, it is to their everlasting credit that the majority of collectors buy for the love of books alone. They buy to hold rather than in expectation that some day a profit may result from the sale of their library. It is an interest that transcends death, members of this sincere group frequently making provision for suitably housing, endowing, and turning over to the inter-

BOOKS ABOUT BOOKS

ests of students and another generation of collectors the books that represent the efforts of a lifetime of collecting.

Men and their habits change but little throughout the ages. Quite probably a consideration of no other subject would bring this fact more forcibly to the attention of the reader than a general perusal of the history of book collecting. From the time of Richard de Bury (1281-1345) whose PHILOBIBLON was the first widely read treatise on bibliography and collecting by an English writer, down to the present day with such popular creators of books on collecting as Mr. A. Edward Newton, Mr. John T. Winterich, Mr. Barton Currie and the late George H. Sargent, there has been a great cumulative interest in books on the part of men in all walks of life.

Victims almost invariably of criticism because of their appreciation of an art beyond the comprehension of many of their associates, book collectors are also more frequently misunderstood than encouraged in the pursuit of their hobby by the members of their immediate family. There has been hardly a book-collector who, at one time or another in the pursuit of his vocation, has not had to smuggle a choice volume into his own house under his coat or in an inside pocket out of sight of the critical eyes of his wife. Poor wretch, as Samuel Pepys, himself a great collector, might say, she cannot understand why so much good money should be spent on books that otherwise might go into furniture, an automobile, or clothes which in her mind are far more important than any book ever printed. It is not fair, of course, that any woman should be deprived of what, to her, are the joys of life in favor of a book, but, after all, no matter what her virtues, a woman has yet to outlive, in fact or in desirability, a Shakespeare folio!

The world owes much, both individually and collectively, to the book collector who has carried on his work. There is not a country which is not visited by some student or collector because of the library or special collection of books it houses. The continued existence of such collections is usually due solely to the faithful pursuit in years past of some collector and the careful stewardship of a succession of capable librarians. In our own country, the J. P. Morgan Library in New York City and the Huntington Library in San Marino, California are perfect examples. It is interesting indeed to consider that whereas the cash, securities, real estate and other property left to the heirs of these two great American business men who were leaders in their respective fields of finance and railroading might easily have been dissipated by falling markets

BOOK COLLECTING AND BOOKS ABOUT BOOKS

if not through carelessness, the books they collected and left in trust can never be lost. Ages hence they will still be available to whoever may care to read of periods in the development of the world of which little may remain except the written record as contained in a manuscript or in a book deposited within these libraries.

While the bibliophile is not usually unduly concerned with the cash value of his books today as compared with what they cost him, yet he is in most instances enough of a business man and has sufficient pride in his ability as an amateur bookman to want the items in his library to hold their own at least and not depreciate in value over a period of years. Of more importance to the collector, however, is the insistence that his books be exactly as represented. Unfortunately, every collector cannot likewise be a scholar, although there are many instances in which he is a far better authority on his particular subject than any individual dealer.

Let us take a hypothetical case. Here is Mr. A, President of the Blank Motors Corporation, an outstanding figure in American industry and finance. He has retained an inborn love of books and, as his wealth increases, finds it possible to gratify his interest in, say, the first editions of early American authors. He sees Ralph Waldo Emerson's CONDUCT OF LIFE, Boston, 1860, listed in a catalogue at twenty dollars. The assumption is that the book is a first edition. In fact, the catalogue says it is. But can Mr. A be certain that twenty dollars is a fair price? Has this particular item the original stamped cloth and does the lettering on the spine correspond with the arrangement that Mr. Richard Curle, author of that admirable volume, FISHERS OF BOOKS, considers to be the correct and original binding? This copy the catalogue states has the necessary sixteen pages of publisher's endorsements, dated December 1860. But what about the binding? As a matter of fact, is Mr. Curle himself correct in his assumption that the lettering on the spine of a first edition should read, EMERSON'S/WRITINGS/CONDUCT OF LIFE./?

Mr. A's real business is the making of motor cars, and, while he has a genuine interest in the subject matter of the books he is collecting, reading as well as purchasing them, yet he has neither the time nor the inclination, perhaps, to make a thorough study of this or other items he contemplates buying. Naturally, he turns to his dealer, but does the dealer know? Selling as he does in the course of a year thousands of different books, is it to be expected that, no matter how good his intentions, the dealer can certify the authenticity of each

9

BOOKS ABOUT BOOKS

individual item that leaves his shelves? Even though a dealer might guarantee an item to be a first edition, he runs a chance of error, although, in all fairness, it must be said that ninety-nine out of one hundred dealers will immediately refund the purchase price if the buyer questions ever so slightly the identity of any book sold him. After all, however, the rare book dealer must be a good business man if he is to stay in business, and he has as his immediate task the job of turning his stock as rapidly as possible.

Probably one of the greatest barriers to his complete enjoyment of the game which the book collector has to face is the apparent lack of an unbiased source from which he can secure reliable and complete data on the particular field of collecting or individual items in which he is interested. There is no agency to which collectors, libraries, associations, administrators of estates or even dealers and others who are concerned with books can turn for advice as regards the rarity, value or other bibliographical details of the books they own or contemplate buying. The collector who lives in one of the larger cities will have a public library at his disposal which he may consult, but, except for a few favored instances, he is even then without expert assistance. Filled though a library may be with such information as is needed to settle or define a bibliographical point, the assistance of one with technical knowledge is needed to find it, and usually when found a further problem arises—that of rendering it into such form as may be intelligible to the average collector.

The collecting of books, if undertaken with the aim of purchasing only those books that are appropriate to one's purpose, is not quite so simple a hobby as it may appear. Gradually, of course, every collector who sticks to one particular subject or author eventually becomes more or less of an authority. Except for individuals of wealth and leisure, however, it would seem almost impossible for the average collector to form the contacts necessary to perform accurate bibliographical research work. Furthermore, even though he might know of some other collector who has specialized in his own or some closely allied phase of collecting, most individuals would hesitate, lacking a personal acquaintance, to write for such information or assistance as might be required.

Writers who carry on columns devoted to rare books in newspapers and magazines are frequently the recipients of questions which they are incapable of answering. Consequently, they excuse themselves from direct reply on the ground that they cannot be bothered by requests of the nature made them. This is but natural, for the average paragrapher is simply a reporter who records the prices

BOOK COLLECTING AND BOOKS ABOUT BOOKS

books have brought at auctions, notes the contents of the dealers' and collectors' catalogues, and reviews books within the field of collecting. Both individually and collectively, however, the contribution they make to bibliographical knowledge is negligible. There are exceptions, of course. One is the late George W. Sargent who for so many years conducted his column, "The Bibliographer," in the *Boston Evening Transcript*. There are others living also who are decidedly not in the hack writer's class. Nevertheless, even with such assistance as they can give, the collector still lacks a proper source for advice, counsel, reliable data and the technical assistance needed if he is to be safe in what is today a highly organized business in which even the smartest of dealers and the most studious collectors are not infrequently caught with their eyes closed.

It is time that some individual or coöperative attempt was made to establish a central source of authority with branches both in this country and abroad which could be consulted by book buyers and book sellers alike. Such branches might be represented by libraries, societies and persons who were rated the highest in their respective bibliographical fields. Famous collections, book clubs and other original sources should be visited in the interest of the collector. The distinguishing characteristics of his own volumes could then be compared with known true copies which only such sources could furnish. Foreign investigation both in England and on the Continent would likewise be essential. Lacking any such organized source of information, however, it is largely necessary for the collector to become his own authority and, before making any serious attempt at collecting, to acquire and peruse diligently books, catalogues and bibliographies pertaining to his special field of endeavor as well as to the larger field of book collecting in general.

In the last analysis, the collector has no one to whom he can turn for reliable or unbiased information. He stands alone on an island of doubt and must dig out for himself or discover from the writings of others the information that will enable him to collect wisely and even, perhaps, profitably. A search of the subject and author files of almost any of the larger public, university or college libraries will reveal relatively few items pertaining to book collecting and bibliography. Some of the modern writers who have chosen to discuss the topic from a popular point of view may be represented, but the bibliographical writers of even a decade ago are conspicuous by their absence. What are the sources of information for the book collector? Not necessarily the dry bibliographical reference manuals, although, of course, they have their place and are

11

BOOKS ABOUT BOOKS

at times indispensible, but rather the text books of the science which the art of book collecting might well be called.

Harold Child, writing in the BIBLIOPHILE'S ALMANAC FOR 1927, says that books about books "are not books in the bibliophile's sense but go to one of them to look up a fact and they have you by the hair, you come to hours later." In reality, these books should be the backbone of any collector's library, for without their assistance, no true knowledge of the art of collecting is possible. The ownership of books of this kind and a study of their contents will give the collector a sound fundamental knowledge, much entertainment and a broad view of the greater portion of the field embraced within the science of book collecting. These books do not have a wide circulation. Listed infrequently in dealers' catalogues, it might safely be said that they are becoming scarce. Nor are these books often found in the auction room although when they are placed under the hammer they invariably bring good prices. As a matter of fact, they are by no means a cheap class of books as a study of the prices obtained at the Eames sales of 1905-1907 and in the Trumbell Reference Library sale in March 1928 will show. Most books within this classification were issued in small editions and have not been reprinted. A collector could do far worse than add a careful selection of these source books to his library for they are practically indispensible to the booklover who, regardless of his major interest, must sooner or later refer to them for guidance.

These books about books have a definite appeal for the booklover, and most collectors have at least a small shelf of them. They are not, however, generally collected. The list of book collectors' specialties, as compiled in PRIVATE BOOK-COLLECTORS, published every three years by R. R. Bowker Company, rarely indicates more than three or four names out of a total of several thousand collectors who are interested in this subject. Probably the greatest single collection of books about books is that housed in the Grolier Club of New York City. Collectors when in this city should by all means see the library of this club. Permission may be obtained from the secretary or librarian. References on every subject associated with books and collecting makes the Grolier Club Library the most complete book club in the world.

Regardless of a collector's specialty, there are certain books which not only contain a great deal of information but which evoke thought and renew enthusiasm, should the reader be in need of encouragement. Each year sees an increase in the number of "popular" books concerning some phase of book collecting.

BOOK COLLECTING AND BOOKS ABOUT BOOKS

By far the majority of these extol, under the guise of an assumed modesty, the author's ability to find and buy a particular book at his own profit and at the loss of the seller. Furthermore, most of these collector authors are riding some particular author or subject hobby. For example, Mr. A. Edward Newton writes of his Johnson and Trollope collections; Dr. A. S. W. Rosenbach, about his Children's Books; Barton Currie, of his Dickens and Thackeray collections.

There is no gainsaying the fact that these books on collecting make interesting reading and serve to whet the appetite of both the new and old collector. There must always be a question in the mind of the reader, however, as to how much the success of these collectors depends upon their bibliographical knowledge and how much upon a fat pocketbook. It is remarkable that so few contributions to the literature of book collecting have been made by authors in modest circumstances. This volume, thanks to the courage of the publishers, is the result of an attempt on the part of a booklover in this category to make some small addition to the existing literature on collecting and at the same time to call attention to a class of books which, while not exactly cheap, are yet out of the class of the first editions which so many other writers have chosen to describe. Collecting in the field of bibliography as outlined in the second chapter of this book will enable the bookman to acquire, while exercising his hobby, a well rounded, fundamental knowledge of the art of book collecting. One reason, perhaps, for the apparent failure on the part of the average collector to write and seek publication of a paper on his activities may lie in the fact that he owns little, if anything, worth bragging about. His purchases are necessarily subject to his means and often made at wide intervals. It is not for him to write of buying a Grey's ELEGY for $5000 and four years later selling it for $12,000!

In an admirable foreword to his Twenty-fifth Anniversary Catalogue, the late Ernest Dresell North, a good bookman and one of the deans of the rare book trade in New York City, mentions the great advance that took place from 1907 to 1927 in the scientific study of bibliography. He further states, "The tools of the collector are much more numerous and accurate than in former days."

Unquestionably this is true. The collector of twenty-five years ago, especially the young student of book collecting, was considerably handicapped through lack of any text books or general literature on the subject, although at that time, Dibdin's influence was still being felt and Slater with his EARLY EDITIONS, THE ROMANCE OF BOOK-COLLECTING, and HOW TO COLLECT BOOKS was the popu-

BOOKS ABOUT BOOKS

lar A. Edward Newton of his day. Drake also says that, when he first entered business in 1902, "there were only two or three books that could be put into the hands of the inquiring collector." He mentions only a single title, Burton's BOOK HUNTER. Coming a bit nearer the present day, he speaks of booksellers who "have been tempted to authorship by the enthusiasm of their customers." Of these, however, he cites only two, namely, Walter T. Spencer and Charles J. Sawyer.

There is still a scarcity of books pertaining to book collecting although during the past several years a number of interesting items have been added to the general list. A. Edward Newton who started the ball rolling in 1918 with his AMENITIES OF BOOK COLLECTING and who is probably the most widely known author in the field has done excellent work in the dissemination of information relative to book selling, Eighteenth Century Literature, and modern English and American first editions. Newton, together with Orcutt and Winterich, to mention but a few of the current authors of books about books, were responsible, as they must be in many other cases, for the present writer's interest in the general subject of book collecting. What author or subject to collect, however, presented a disturbing problem. The conclusion was gradually reached that, after all, perhaps the first step might properly consist in acquiring some knowledge of the fundamental principles upon which the art of successful collecting must depend.

The belief was strengthened by the desire to assemble books which, in their well rounded relationship to one another, would be worthy of being called a library. After all, a real library is far removed from the mere acquisition of a collection of books which, only too often, are bought with an eye on rising prices rather than with the intention of accumulating a series of items valuable, aside from their intrinsic worth, for illustrating some phase in the development of the world's literature or describing the part played by some individual or group of writers in its growth.

Once made, this decision proved invaluable, for it brought forcibly to the author's attention the lack in public libraries of the text books or "tools" which the collector might wish to consult. Furthermore, letters to well known collectors requesting suggestions as to what texts should be studied with a view to acquiring a preliminary training before beginning the more serious work of actual collecting, brought forth, in a majority of instances, only the mention of the latest popular book on the subject.

BOOK COLLECTING AND BOOKS ABOUT BOOKS

Realizing finally that any real information on the principles of book collecting and bibliography must come very largely as a result of self effort, the writer has attempted to collect such literature in English which might serve as a practical working library for the inexperienced collector. The dealer as well might profitably enlarge his own reference library as much as his resources permit, for the volume of his business is bound to increase in direct proportion to his bibliographical knowledge.

This book, therefore, in the pages which immediately follow, is a first attempt to describe a few of the books and articles on bibliography and collecting which should be of most interest and value to the bookman.

CHAPTER II

The Bio-Bibliography

To many readers a bibliography represents hardly more than the dry reading of a list of books upon a given subject or author. A bibliography can and should mean much more than this. The writer has, therefore, striven to emulate his mentor, Sir William Osler, who said, "What more arid than long lists of titles—what more fascinating, on the other hand, the story of the book as part of the life of the man who wrote it—the bio-bibliography."

Again quoting Osler, "A library represents the mind of its collector, his fancies and foibles, his strength and weakness, his prejudices and preferences. Particularly is this the case if to the character of a collector he adds—or tries to add—the qualities of a student who wishes to know the books and the lives of the men who wrote them." Thus is so ably expressed the intent of the writer in presenting upon the following pages some of the books from his own collection.

No claim is made for bibliographical completeness. Rather, there are given descriptions sufficient only to identify the various books herein listed and to arouse the interest of the reader in them.

The prices that have been affixed in this Bio-Bibliographical Section will undoubtedly occasion comment from dealers and collectors alike. In the main, they represent the prices paid for the writer's own books, but in certain instances where no records were kept the figures given are very close to present day values.

Books about books—and by that is not meant bibliographies of authors or subjects but, rather, in the main classifications, books relating to book collecting and the science of bibliography—are becoming scarce. They are not met with in any quantity upon booksellers' shelves and prices asked for them show a tendency to rise. Many of these books were printed in limited numbers, and the bookman who recognizes the need for a reference library before beginning active collecting would do well to select early in his career the items in this category which he will need as guides.

THE BIO-BIBLIOGRAPHY

Adams, Randolph G. (1892-   )

> THE WHYS AND WHEREFORES OF THE WILLIAM L. CLEMENTS LIBRARY, a Brief Essay on Book-Collecting as a Fine Art. 8vo, grey boards, one of 200 copies. Alumni Press, University of Michigan, 1925.
>
> $3.00

This essay was adapted from an interview with Mr. Adams, Librarian of the William L. Clements Library at Ann Arbor, Michigan. It first appeared in the *Michigan Daily* of May 24, 1925. While it was intended, as Mr. Adams states in his Foreword, as a "brief interpretation of the library," yet it is in the main a tribute to the great book collectors. It reveals Mr. Adams not only as a true lover of old books but as a librarian who understands his job, his relations to those who seek his assistance and the assistance of the volumes within his charge; and also as a man of vision and sympathy for collecting as an art and for collectors as individuals.

Every collector should read this monograph if only for its inspirational content. That Mr. Adams understands the soul of the average collector is witnessed by his statement, "I wish some industrious person would write a book on the immense debt that civilization owes to the man who amasses books, if he never does anything else." "Few people," he says, "are interested in collecting unimportant books—the mind of the collector is essentially sympathetic and imaginative. He sees without logical processes the importance of a book before the patient investigator finds the reason for its importance. In a very real sense, the collector frequently foresees the importance of a book before the writer of a dissertation thereon—indeed the investigator probably never would see the book if the collector had not rescued it."

Allen, P. B. M.

> THE BOOK HUNTER AT HOME. 8vo, grey boards, cloth back, t.e.g., uncut, large paper, limited to 500 copies, four plates, second and finest edition. London, 1922.
>
> $12.30

The first edition was published in London in 1920 and can be bought for about $7.50. The first American edition was issued in New York in the same year, bound in blue cloth, and is worth $5.00. There was also a second American edition published in New York in 1922.

BOOKS ABOUT BOOKS

This is an admirable book, interestingly presenting a wide variety of facts. Among the chapters are: "Adventures Among Books," "Care of Books," "What to Collect," etc. One chapter of thirty-four pages is devoted to "Books of the Collector," in other words, reference books or books about books. It is interesting to note the extent to which the field was covered at the time of the publication.

Allen's fine list of works, either in English or in translation, for the book collector who would at the outset provide himself with the volumes necessary for obtaining a working knowledge of his avocation include:

1.	Burton's	BOOK HUNTER
2.	Blade's	ENEMIES OF BOOKS
3.	Blade's	LIFE AND TYPOGRAPHY OF WILLIAM CANTON
4.	Lang's	THE LIBRARY
5.	Lang's	BOOKS AND BOOKMEN
6.	Harrison's	CHOICE OF BOOKS
7.	Harrison's	AMONG MY BOOKS
8.	Clark's	CARE OF BOOKS
9.	Edwards'	LIBRARIES AND FOUNDERS OF LIBRARIES
10.	Duff's	EARLY PRINTED BOOKS
11.	Duff's	THE PRINTERS OF WESTMINSTER AND LONDON TO 1535
12.	Duff's	ENGLISH PROVINCIAL PRINTERS
13.	Bradshaw's	COLLECTED PAPERS
14.	Pollard's	EARLY ILLUSTRATED BOOKS
15.	Wheatley's	PRICES OF BOOKS
16.	Ferguson's	ASPECTS OF BIBLIOGRAPHY
17.	Bibliographical	SOCIETY PUBLICATIONS
18.	Lownde's	BIBLIOGRAPHER'S MANUAL
19.	Hazlitt's	BIBLIOGRAPHICAL COLLECTIONS AND NOTES ON EARLY ENGLISH LITERATURE
20.	Arber's	TERM CATALOGUES
21.	Brydge's	BRITISH BIBLIOGRAPHER
22.	Brydge's	CENSURA LITERARIA
23.	Brydge's	RESTITUTA OR TITLES, EXTRACTS AND CHARACTERS OF OLD BOOKS IN ENGLISH LITERATURE REVIVED
24.	Collier's	ACCOUNT OF THE RAREST BOOKS IN THE ENGLISH LANGUAGE
25.	Karslake's	NOTES FROM SOTHERBY'S
26.	Quaritch's	GENERAL CATALOGUE OF BOOKS
27.	Huth Library	CATALOGUE

THE BIO-BIBLIOGRAPHY

28. British Museum	CATALOGUE OF BOOKS TO 1640
29.	DICTIONARY OF NATIONAL BIOGRAPHY
30.	CAMBRIDGE HISTORY OF ENGLISH LITERATURE
31. Allibone's	CRITICAL DICTIONARY OF ENGLISH LITERATURE AND AMERICAN AUTHORS
32. Hain's	REPERTORIUM BIBLIOGRAPHICUM
33. Sayle's	LIST OF EARLY ENGLISH PRINTED BOOKS IN THE UNIVERSITY LIBRARY, CAMBRIDGE, 1475-1640
34. Madam's	THE EARLY OXFORD PRESS
35. Proctor's	INDEX TO THE EARLY PRINTED BOOKS IN THE BRITISH MUSEUM FROM THE INVENTION OF PRINTING TO THE YEAR MD
36. British Museum	A CATALOGUE OF BOOKS PRINTED IN THE FIFTEENTH CENTURY
37. Sotherby's	PRINCIPIA TYPOGRAPHY
38. Bigmore and Wyman's	BIBLIOGRAPHY OF PRINTING
39. Sargent and Whishaw's	GUIDE BOOK TO BOOKS
40. Bibliography Society	BIBLIOGRAPHICA
41. Halkett and Laing's	DICTIONARY OF THE ANONYMOUS AND PSEUDONYMOUS LITERATURE OF GREAT BRITAIN
42. Dibden's	TYPOGRAPHICAL ANTIQUITIES
43. Dibden's	BIBLIOGRAPHICAL DECAMERON
44. Sabin's	BIBLIOGRAPHY OF BIBLIOGRAPHIES
45. Courtney's	REGISTER OF NATIONAL BIBLIOGRAPHY
46. Wheatley's	PRICES OF BOOKS
47. Pretsholdt's	BIBLIOTHICA BIBLIOGRAPHICA

The above list of reference books picked out of Allen's chapter on "Books for the Collector" is of considerable value to the bookman interested in bibliography and in books about books. The list will bear being reproduced here and is done so with no apologies to the original compiler but rather with congratulations on its completeness.

This list and the text of Allen's entire chapter, "Books for the Collector," is typical of the practical usefulness of THE BOOK HUNTER AT HOME. It might well be the first among the books described here for the reader to acquire who is about to begin the collecting of books. It is a very satisfying introductory work to the exciting adventure of book collecting in all its various phases. As Allen himself says, "To the real collector, there is no more delightful reading than the literature which deals with the subject he has made his own; and the more ample and specialized it be, the greater will be his delight."

BOOKS ABOUT BOOKS

Andrews, William Loring (1837-1920)

GOSSIP ABOUT BOOK COLLECTING. 12 full page illustrations, some in color. 2 vols., 8vo, decorated covers, gilt top. 125 copies on Holland Paper. New York, 1900.

$40.00

The same, 32 copies on Japan paper, $150.00

This is a beautiful and scarce book. Another edition printed on Japan paper in the same year was limited to 32 copies and priced at $165. William Loring Andrews was a famous collector and the author of some thirty-five fascinating and expensive books on collecting and allied subjects. All of his books are not only intensely interesting to the bookman, but are beautifully printed as well. They are a lasting monument to his character and taste.

During his lifetime he assembled a large collection of books which he sold shortly before his death on March 20, 1920 to the late James P. Drake, the well known New York dealer. Mr. Andrews was a founder of the Grolier Club, its second president, and for many years a trustee of the Metropolitan Museum of Art. He was founder and the only president of the Society of Iconophiles in the name of which many of his books were issued.

American Book Collector, The

A Monthly Magazine for Book Lovers, devoted to Bibliography and Americana, numerous illustrations. Metuchen, New Jersey, 1925-1935.

Per Year, $5.00

It seems to be a difficult task to maintain in this country a book collector's magazine. Among those that have been given birth, only to succumb eventually from lack of subscriptions or advertising support, are: THE BOOKLOVER, THE BIBLIOPHILIST, THE LITERARY COLLECTOR, and THE BIBLIOGRAPHER. The most successful publication in this field to date was THE AMERICAN BOOK COLLECTOR, founded by Mr. Charles F. Heartman.

Mr. Heartman, who holds frequent book auctions at Metuchen, New Jersey, is a man of considerable energy and enthusiasm for book collecting and bibliography. In addition, he is the author of many articles on these subjects. The purpose of his publication was to present an unbiased account of the events occurring in the field of book collecting and to provide as well a medium for sound and accurate articles of a bibliographical nature. It proved a very useful magazine, devoted entirely to the interests of collectors and booklovers. It was always worth its subscription price and collectors who failed to subscribe should try and purchase a complete set through some second hand dealer. Unfortunately, in June 1935 the publishers announced that the magazine would not appear between July and December. They hoped by January 1, 1936 to produce a new series. To date this has not appeared. Subscribers received their choice of a cash rebate or a copy of Heartman's book, NON-NEW ENGLAND PRIMER, in return for their unexpired subscriptions.

American Book Prices Current

AMERICAN BOOK PRICES CURRENT. An annual record of book auction sales in the United States arranged alphabetically by author and title. 8vo, red buckram. Dodd, Mead & Company; Dodd Livingston Company; E. P. Dutton Company; R. R. Bowker Company, New York, 1895-1937.

Annual Volumes, $20.00
Complete Set, $185-200

First compiled in 1895 by Luther S. Livingston and published by Dodd, Mead and Company of New York. For forty years these yearly volumes containing a record of books, manuscripts, and autographs sold at auction in this country, together with the prices realized, have offered a handy and accurate source of information from which to estimate in any one year the probable value of many thousands of rare books. In addition, the volumes provide an interesting record of the development of the rare book trade in this country. Mr. Livingston, who was a distinguished bibliographer, edited prior to his death twenty of the yearly volumes.

In 1910 their publication was taken over by the newly organized firm of Dodd Livingston, which continued to issue them until 1914, when E. P. Dutton Company, upon the retirement of Mr. Livingston to become Librarian of the Widener Memorial Library at Harvard, acquired the publication rights.

Each new volume as issued sells for $20.00 and is well worth the money. Second hand copies usually cost from $2.50 up depending upon condition and the year of publication. Of volume one only 400 copies were printed in the first edition, and during the first year 550 copies were issued, this number gradually increasing to 900 copies. The 1934-35 volume was issued in an edition of 700 copies. The early volumes are scarce and it is difficult to complete a set. Even the present number, printed each year, seems rather small if all dealers, let alone libraries and collectors, are to be supplied. It is generally considered that they are more accurate, and the auction prices quoted represent a better picture of the actual value of the books included than is the case in ENGLISH BOOK AUCTION RECORDS published in London.

While a complete set of AMERICAN BOOK PRICES CURRENT, with Index representing to date 42 volumes, would take up considerable shelf room and cost in the neighborhood of $185-$200, yet the collector—who is to make any pretense of being at the same time a student of his hobby—should have constantly at hand this cumulative record of the prices that the books he is interested in have brought during the current and preceding years.

The Index, 1916-1922, published in 1925, contains 1,397 pages and lists nearly 100,000 items. The published price was $30.00 for each copy in an edition of 750 copies. Unsold volumes were at one time offered by the publishers at $5.00.

On September 1, 1929 the publication of AMERICAN BOOK PRICES CURRENT, then in its thirty-fourth year, was assumed by R. R. Bowker Company of New York City. This firm is continuing, under the editorship of Mary Houston Warren, the same high standard of bibliographical excellence to which subscribers to the volumes are accustomed.

The physical labor and details involved in a work of this kind are almost overwhelming. From priced auction catalogues each item is card indexed and sorted. Books that sell for less than $7.50 are eliminated. Great care is taken for accuracy of bibliographical description and, when necessary, known authoritative sources are carefully checked. Naturally, the task of having each entry correct takes many months and delay in publication is inevitable at times.

Anonyma and Pseudonyma

ANONYMA AND PSEUDONYMA, a Complete Dictionary by Charles A. Stonehill, Jr., Andrew Block and H. Winthrop Stonehill, Containing a condensed description and key of over 35,000 books from the beginning of printing in England until June 1926. 4 vols., 8vo, cloth. New York.

$7.50

THE BIO-BIBLIOGRAPHY

This reference work was first published at $25.00, but in 1933 R. R. Bowker Company issued the reduced edition described above. It is probably the most complete and indispensable work of its kind ever published. The system employed enables one to identify 100,000 different books or almost treble the number actually described. It is understood that in compiling these volumes every work on anonymous literature was consulted and some 500 separate bibliographies studied. Extracts were also taken from over 3000 English and American booksellers' catalogues.

Antiquarian Magazine and Bibliographer, The

> THE ANTIQUARIAN MAGAZINE AND BIBLIOGRAPHER, edited by E. Walford. 8vo, boards, cloth back, gilt, t.e.g. 7 vols. London, 1882-1885.
>
> $15.00

The writer, being attracted by the title, purchased this item in a Washington, D. C. book store some years ago. It is included as an example of what not to buy and as a warning not to be fooled by titles. A few book reviews and descriptions of library sales were published in this magazine, but unless some present day collector is interested in chronicles of the meetings of learned English societies, he must look elsewhere for his bibliographical information.

Arber, Edward (1836-1912)

> THE TERM CATALOGUES, 1668-1709 A.D. A Contemporary Bibliography of English Literature in the Reigns of Charles II, James II, William, Mary and Anne; 3 volumes. Imperial 4to, large paper, limited to 100 copies. Privately printed, London, 1903-06.
>
> $35.00

This monumental bibliography of Arber's was printed in two editions. The large paper in royal quarto consisted of 100 numbered copies and the small paper edition in demy quarto comprised 2000 copies. Both editions are signed by the author.

This is an essential work for all collectors and bibliographers interested in the period 1668-1709. Arber has been generous in his descriptions and even the collector who is not particularly concerned with Early English Literature, will find a great deal of interesting reading in these volumes. An evening spent in turning the pages of this great bibliography might be passed by a bookman in a far less entertaining way. The three volumes completely justify the shelf room they occupy.

THE TERM CATALOGUES are the official lists of new books and new editions printed in England during the periods indicated by each issue. Like the earlier RECORDS OF THE STATIONER'S COMPANY, also edited by Arber, they are a most complete record of books published during a very prolific period in the development of English literature. The large paper edition was originally priced at $140.00 and the ordinary edition at $70.00.

Arnold, William Harris (1854-1923)

> FIRST REPORT OF A BOOK-COLLECTOR, Comprising a Brief Answer to the Frequent Question, "Why First Editions?" and Five Egotistical Chapters of Anecdote and Advice Addressed to the Beginner in Book-Collecting. Facsimilies and folding plates, small folio, vellum, cloth library case. First edition, 85 copies printed at the Marion Press, New York, 1897-8.
> $65.00

William Harris Arnold was a professional bookman and throughout his life a leading figure in the trade. Having organized Wanamaker's book department for the first time in the early eighties, he remained active in the handling of books until his death in 1923.

Arnold was also a great book collector, showing taste and skill in acquiring a large and varied collection. Many of his books were bought only to be sold again during his lifetime. At his death there remained over 1000 volumes each indicative of his personal taste and interest. These books were sold at auction in the Anderson Galleries on November 10-11, 1924. Mr. R. B. Adam of Buffalo, the great Johnsonian, wrote a delightful preface to the catalogue.

Arnold, William Harris (1854-1923)

> RECORD OF AMERICAN FIRST EDITIONS, with an Essay on Book-Madness by Leon H. Vincent. 4to, blue cloth, paper label, 24 copies on Japan paper. New York, 1901.
> $30.00

Mr. Arnold again describes his activities as a collector but in this instance the record is confined to early American authors, namely, Bryant, Emerson,

Hawthorne, Holmes, Longfellow, Lowell, Thoreau and Whittier. Some 709 items were purchased within a period of six years for $3508.16 and sold for $7363.17, with a resulting profit of $3855.01.

It must be remembered that Arnold's investments in books were made some thirty-four years ago when prices were much lower than they are today. A comparison of retail and actual sale prices for many of the individual items he mentions would show an even more rapid rate of increase in value in recent years. It is useless to attempt to give any comparative figures today for the items included in Arnold's collection as we have no means of considering their present condition or other factors which play such an important part in determining the price any book will bring.

A feature of this book which does much to excuse its mercenary content is Leon H. Vincent's introductory essay. This is a real contribution to the literature of book collecting and well worth reading. It adds much to the simple records that follow of mere cost and selling prices. To the bibliophile, and in this instance the term "collector" is not used, for anyone may be a collector, any outward boast of profits resulting from the sale of his books is decidedly bad form, even though Arnold presents the results of his collecting activities in quiet good taste and lets the figures speak for themselves.

Arnold, William Harris (1854-1923)

A RECORD OF BOOKS AND LETTERS with an Essay on the Collector's Point of View by Leon H. Vincent. 4to, red cloth, paper label, 29 copies, on Japan paper. New York, 1901.

$30.00
As above. 116 copies on hand made paper, $15.00

In his introduction Vincent is quite explicit in his description of what any contribution to the history of prices of rare books should include. Speaking of Arnold's compilation he says, "It shows for what sums of money an astute collector has been able to buy not a few of the most desirable things that ever came upon the market; it also shows at how considerable an advance over the purchase price such treasures may be sold."

Arnold's book is a valuable record of the cost and selling prices of rare books and letters and with its companion volume, RECORD OF AMERICAN FIRST EDI-

TIONS, issued earlier in the same year, might well be cited by any collector in defense of his hobby when the dollar and cents value of his book collecting efforts are questioned.

In this book Arnold records the collecting of some 411 miscellaneous first editions, including certain of the Kelmscott Press books, at a total cost of $10,066.05. This collection he sold within six years for $19,743.50 thus enjoying a profit of $9,677.45.

Anyone who knew Arnold, however, would realize that his greatest pleasure and profit came from collecting and owning these books rather than from the capital increase he enjoyed at their sale.

Arnold, William Harris (1854-1923)

VENTURES IN BOOK COLLECTING. 8vo, boards. New York, 1923.

$1.50

This book as the title suggests is largely autobiographical and tells in entertaining fashion of the experiences of the author in collecting the books he fancied. Arnold completed the manuscript only a few short weeks prior to his death, and it remained to be published by his wife.

Bibliographer, The

THE BIBLIOGRAPHER, A Journal of Book Lore. 6 vols. 4to, cloth, buckram back. Edited by H. B. Wheatley, from December 1881 to November 1884. London, 1882-1884.

$10.00

This Journal was apparently started with the objects in mind of providing current information in a convenient and accessible form, of giving an account of what was going on in the bibliographical world and in providing a medium of communication between those interested in old books.

Unfortunately, its public support was limited, funds for continued publication were difficult to secure, and in December 1884 it was incorporated with BOOK LORE. The lover of old time literature and books, however, will find a great deal of interest in THE BIBLIOGRAPHER for it is illustrative of the activities of English bookmen in the Victorian Era.

Bibliographer, The

THE BIBLIOGRAPHER, A Journal of Bibliography and Rare Book News. Edited by Paul Leicester Ford and published nine months in the year (July, August and September numbers omitted) by Dodd, Mead and Company. Numerous portraits and plates. 8vo., gray wrappers. Vols. 1 and 2 (all published). New York, 1902-03.

$25.00

This was an ambitious undertaking but short lived, perhaps because much of its subject material was over the heads of its intended subscription list. There is but little within its contents that would warrant perusal on the part of the modern bookman, yet it definitely dates the period of its publication and, unless the publishers were far off, which they may certainly have been, is indicative of the bibliographical and rare book news of interest to book collectors of thirty-five years ago.

Issued at a subscription price of five dollars per year, the field of books, manuscripts and autographs was ably covered by the editor, Paul Leicester Ford. Many well-known names appear as contributors, among them being William Michael Rossetti, John Boyd Thatcher, Beverly Chew, Henry R. Plomer, George Saintsbury, Wilberforce Eames, William Dana Orcutt, Austin Dobson, Cyril Davenport, Theodore W. Koch and Victor Hugo Paltsits.

A word is in order regarding Mr. Ford, whose untimely death occurred as the May, 1902, issue was about to go to press. His position as editor was not filled by the publishers. He was a scholar, novelist and bibliographer of note, particularly of the Revolutionary period of American history and bibliography.

Bibliographica

BIBLIOGRAPHICA—PAPERS ON BOOKS, THEIR HISTORY AND ART, by Andrew Lang, Austin Dobson, Sir Sidney Lee, Richard Garnett, Sir E. Maude Thompson, E. Arber, and others. Sixty-five fine plates, facsimiles from ancient manuscripts, early printed books and bindings, 12 parts in 3 vols., imperial 8vo, half morocco, t.e.g. London 1893-97.

$45.00

BOOKS ABOUT BOOKS

A complete set of these papers, unbound, and in twelve parts with wrappers as issued is worth approximately $35. The collection of papers is of the utmost importance in any bibliographical library.

There is probably more information of word for word value in these volumes than in any other collection or writings on Libraries, Bookmen, Booksellers, Early Printing, Bibliography, Book Sales, Prices, Manuscripts, Illustrated Books, Bindings, Book Clubs and Book Plates. For a general outline that covers, to some extent at least, all of the ramifications of book collecting, the beginner could hardly secure a better understanding of his hobby than to read these fascinating papers from beginning to end. After the first reading, let him go back and do it all over again! This procedure may be necessary, for fully half of the contents are of a highly technical character, but there is a sufficiency of popular articles profusely illustrated with reproductions, illustrated pages, bindings, colophons, title pages, etc., which no collector, however slight his experience, will find difficult. If a perusal of these volumes does nothing more than increase one's working vocabulary, the time involved in their study will be well spent.

Bibliographia Series

BIBLIOGRAPHIA SERIES, edited by Michael Sadlier, comprising Points in Eighteenth Century Poetry by I. A. Williams, Binding Variants by John Carter, Bibliography of the Waverly Novels, by Grenville Worthington, Bibliography of William Beckford by Grey Chapman, Cancels by R. W. Chapman, Evolution of Binding Styles by Michael Sadlier, Points, 1870-1930 and Points, Second Series 1866-1934 by Percy H. Muir. Anglo-American Editions, 8 vols. London, 1930-1937. $50.00

Of the above eight volumes in the SERIES as published to date, EVOLUTION OF BINDING STYLES by Michael Sadlier, and POINTS, 1870-1930, by Percy H. Muir are out of print. Additions to these contributions to book history and book structure are to be made from time to time. The individual authors are experts in their respective fields and may be read with much profit. The pure bibliographies in the SERIES will not have much interest except to the chance collector interested in the particular authors whose works are so carefully described. Mr. Muir's POINTS, Mr. Carter's BINDING VARIANTS and Mr. Chapman's CANCELS are, however, essential to the education of all collectors. The individual volumes are attractively bound and printed. The SERIES should not be broken up.

Bibliographical Society of America

THE PAPERS OF THE BIBLIOGRAPHICAL SOCIETY OF AMERICA.
University of Chicago Press, Chicago, Illinois, 1908.
Each, $2.00

The Bibliographical Society of America was founded and incorporated in 1904 and has met semi-annually since that date. Its purpose is the production of bibliographical research and the printing of resulting papers. The yearly PAPERS of the Society which are issued as funds become available for their printing, are of considerable value to book collectors. Anyone interested in the object of the Society and approved by the Council may become a member upon payment of the dues which are $3.00 a year. Information may be secured from the Secretary, Mr. Augustus H. Shearer, Librarian of the Grosvenor Library, Buffalo, New York.

At least one number of the Society's PAPERS is published annually. There are available from the Society or the Chicago University Press, numbers for the years 1906 and 1907, 1910 to and including 1922, and 1925 to the current year's volume.

AN INDEX TO THE PUBLICATIONS OF THE BIBLIOGRAPHICAL SOCIETY OF AMERICA, 1889-1931, (vols. I-XXV) has been published. The price is $2.00 for members and $2.50 for non-members.

Bibliophile Society (Boston)

YEAR BOOKS, Bibliophile Society, Boston. Splendidly illustrated with many fine plates, 8vo, boards, uncut. Vols. 1-33, Boston, 1902.

$02.50

These volumes, aside from the annual reports of the Society, contain a great deal of interesting and valuable literary material. Much of it is not found elsewhere. There is included much of the heretofore unpublished writing of Longfellow, Whittier, Thoreau and others. Noted bibliophiles including Buxton

BOOKS ABOUT BOOKS

Forman, Brander Matthews, E. C. Stedman, Roswell Field and Adrian H. Joline have contributed a number of articles. Facsimiles of important letters of Poe, Twain, and Field are important features of these books.

Bibliophile, The

THE BIBLIOPHILE, A Magazine for the Collector, Student and General Reader. 4to, 19 parts in orig. wrappers, numerous illustrations and facsimiles. Vols. 1-4 (all published). London, 1908-9.

$12.50

Among the contributors are A. W. Pollard, G. K. Chesterton, R. H. Plomer, and J. H. Slater, who provided articles on printing, bookbinding, and allied topics.

Bibliotheca Anglo-Poetica

BIBLIOTHECA ANGLO-POETICA, A Descriptive Catalogue of a Rare and Rich Collection of Early English Poetry. Boards, paper label. London, 1815.

$25.00

This bibliography is indispensable to the collector of early English Literature. It contains full bibliographical descriptions of 956 rare books with their contemporary valuations. Fifty copies on large paper were also printed. One with illustrations on India Paper and with 40 rare portraits has brought $100. At the Poor Library sale in 1908 the above copy sold for $26.00.

Bierstadt, O. E.

THE LIBRARY OF ROBERT HOE, A Contribution to the History of Bibliophilism in America. One of 350 copies by the DeVinne Press on Japan Paper, 100 illustrations from books and manuscripts in the collection, 8vo, blue cloth, gilt, uncut. New York, 1895.

$20.00

The Hoe Library was noted for its carefully chosen literary masterpieces and this book constitutes a description of certain outstanding rarities. The volume is not of practical value to the average present-day collector although its contents provide a rich background for all bookmen. Because of its discussion of Manuscripts, Incunubula, Aldines, Elzivers and other interesting and important fields, it makes excellent and entertaining reading even though actual participation in most of the branches of book collecting enjoyed by Hoe is open today only to the man of extremely large means.

Birrell, Augustine (1850-1933)

> FREDERICK LOCKER-LAMPSON. 4to, white buckram, gilt top, uncut, portrait and 3 full-page plates. 100 numbered copies signed by the author. London, 1920.
> $7.50

Augustine Birrell who was active in English politics throughout most of his life, holding among other offices that of Minister of Education and Chief Secretary for Ireland, was as well known for his literary endeavors as for his political career. He was the son-in-law of Frederick Locker-Lampson, whose charming personality and library he describes in the above volume.

Birrell's first books of essays, OBITER DICTA, published in 1884 brought him favorable notices from the critics. This was followed by his excellent LIFE OF BRONTE, RES JUDICATAE and MEN, WOMEN AND BOOKS. He also found time to edit Boswell's LIFE OF JOHNSON, to publish biographies of Hazlett and Marvell and to contribute to the literary world of his time many other delightful essays. His great hobby was book collecting and he loved his books for their own sake, as should all true bibliophiles, rather than because of the rarities his library contained.

Locker-Lampson assembled the famous Rowfrant Library and the above volume includes interesting bibliographical notes on a few of its most famous items as well as a selection of letters addressed to this collector.

Blackburn, Charles F.

> RAMBLES IN BOOKS, limited to 500 copies, cr.8vo, portrait on title page, red cloth, gilt. First edition, London, 1893.
> $1.50

This is a personal account of one collector's library with notes covering the reasons for his attraction to many of the books listed. No rarities are described, the catalogue being, without any bibliographical details, a description of Mr.

Blackburn's books as he saw and thought of them. Some of his notes on individual volumes are mildly entertaining but few if any of the items described are of interest to the modern collector. The work is perhaps an example of a "book about books" that was published more for the satisfaction of the author than to the profit of the reader.

Blades, William (1824-1890)

> THE ENEMIES OF BOOKS. 8vo, frontispiece and 6 other plates, decorative parchment wrappers, large paper. First edition, London, 1880.
>
> $12.50
>
> Another copy, revised and enlarged. 8vo, frontispiece and 7 other illustrations, green cloth, gilt. Second edition indexed. One of the Book-Lover's Library, London, 1888.
>
> $1.25

Blades was a prosperous London printer, perhaps the counterpart of Theodore De Vinne in this country. A bookman who devoted considerable time to researches concerning his great predecessor, William Caxton, he was nevertheless interested in all subjects concerning the printed book. This is witnessed by his long series of publications bearing such titles as BOOKS IN CHAINS, THE EARLY SCHOOLS OF TYPOGRAPHY, THE FIRST PRINTING-PRESS IN ENGLAND and many others.

This particular essay in its original form appeared first in the August, September and October numbers of THE PRINTERS' REGISTER for 1879. This was a monthly publication devoted to the interest of printers. As a book for bibliophiles it has, as Blades states in his Preface, "been augmented by much additional matter and many unpublished anecdotes."

The title is a literal one in that the author has dwelt in detail upon the nine destructive "enemies" of books as he sees them in the form of Fire, Water, Gas and Heat, Dust and Neglect, Ignorance, The Bookworm, Other Vermin, Bookbinders and Collectors. The plates form an interesting feature of the book, for they illustrate etching, wood engraving, woodbury type, lithography and photo-typography. Incidentally, the illustrations appearing in the second edition are entirely different. Plate VI is a folded double-page size reproduction entitled "The image of the Booke Worm as it is graven in MICROGRAPHIA by R.

THE BIO-BIBLIOGRAPHY

Hooke, Fellow of the Royal Society, Folio, London, 1665," while Plate V is a double-page spread, photographic reproduction of two leaves of a "Caxton" showing the destruction done by bookworms.

This is an entertaining and informative book. It was evidently written and published with care and is worthy of a prominent place in any collection of books about books.

Block, Andrew (1892-   )

THE BOOK COLLECTOR'S VADE MECUM. 8vo, red cloth, gold title and ornament. London, 1932.

$2.00

This is a rather peculiar book compiled by a London bookseller. Its contents almost wholly comprise lists of books more or less currently popular in the various departments of collecting.

The work is divided into two parts. Book 1 has sixteen chapters in which are mentioned the collector's items that are embraced in modern first editions, rare and early technical works, printing and bibliography, incunubula, science and medicine, sports and pastimes, travel, art books and other branches of collecting activity.

Book II is devoted to the works of Shakespeare and to such other authors as Scott, Leigh Hunt, Shelley, Keats, Byron, Dickens, Thackeray, Ainsworth, Browning and Tennyson. This section is chiefly a check list.

There are two appendices, one devoted to a description of three modern English binders and the other gives brief sketches of a number of prominent London booksellers. This section of the book is perhaps the most interesting for the average reader.

Book Auction Records

BOOK AUCTION RECORDS, a Priced and Annotated Record of London Book Auctions, edited by Frank Karslake. Vol. 1, June 3, 1902 to June 27, 1903.

$23.00

These yearly records are the English companion volumes of AMERICAN BOOK PRICES CURRENT and contain "a priced and annotated record of London book auctions." Prior to 1903 they were known as SALES RECORDS, but the first volume containing some 20,000 items in the new series was compiled by Frank Karslake

BOOKS ABOUT BOOKS

and published by his own company in January 1903. Volume 1 of this new series is extremely interesting and contains four photographs which Karslake called "Pot Shots at Publishers and Others." The above copy is a substantial volume well bound in brown cloth with top, side and bottom edges gilt. Karslake, who died in 1920, left an estate of only £314, and this after twenty years of hard work spent on these records, all of which is indicative of the fact that virtue is its own reward, particularly in the book and publishing business.

In September 1924 the entire interest in the copyright, goodwill and stock of BOOK AUCTION RECORDS were purchased from the estate of Mrs. Karslake by Henry Stevens, Son and Stiles, an important firm of London booksellers. They immediately set to work to bring up to date the compilation of prices which had fallen some six months in arrears and in a little more than two years succeeded in bringing the volumes up to date.

For some time prior to their acquisition by Henry Stevens, Son and Stiles, BOOK AUCTION RECORDS were issued quarterly. This has been continued and the quarterly issues now contain an accurate record of the prices received at London, Edinburgh, Glasgow and Dublin book auctions. Subscription to the Quarterly Parts is at the rate of £1-10s per annum. These parts are exchangeable for the cloth bound volume at the end of the year upon the payment of four shillings more. R. R. Bowker Company of New York City are the American agents for BOOK AUCTION RECORDS which sell in this country for ten dollars a copy.

Frank Karslake, who was also the founder of the International Association of Antiquarian Booksellers, was born in 1851 and died in 1920. About 1892 he came to this country and settled in California, but he was at heart a bookman rather than a farmer. Packing up his possessions, which included nine children, he returned to England and the world of books. He had been apprenticed in 1867 at sixteen years of age to one David White, a London bookseller, and it was inevitable that he should return to his first love.

Book Collecting

NEW PATHS IN BOOK COLLECTING, Essays by Various Hands, edited by John Carter. 8vo, green cloth, gilt. First edition, London, 1934.

$3.50

The contributing authors of this interesting book are John T. Winterich, John Carter, Percy H. Muir, C. B. Oldam, Michael Sadlier, T. Balston, David

THE BIO-BIBLIOGRAPHY

L. Randall and Graham Pollard. They present nine new fields for the collector which include "Detective Fiction," "Musical First Editions," "Yellow Backs," "The Expansion of an Author Collection," "Serials" and "War Books." NEW PATHS IN BOOK COLLECTING is of particular value to the book lover with a modest purse who wishes to become an active collector. Each new generation of collectors needs some new departments for their activities. This book offers excellent suggestions and may give even the satiated collector fresh ideas for his book hunting mind.

Book Collector's Quarterly, The

> THE BOOK COLLECTOR'S QUARTERLY, edited by Desmond Flower and A. J. A. Symons. 8vo, red cloth, gilt, uncut, limited to 100 copies on English hand-made paper. Vols. I-IV. London, Dec. 1930 to Oct. 1931.
> $17.50
> The same, decorative cloth, Vol. V limited to 100 copies, Vols. VI, VII and VIII to 75 copies each. London, Jan. 1932 to Oct. 1932.
> $17.50
> The same, paper wrappers, Vol. IX Jan. 1933 to ——
> per year, $4.50

THE BOOK COLLECTOR'S QUARTERLY is the official organ of the First Edition Club of London. This club is an international association of bibliophiles, membership of which is open to accredited collectors. The purpose of the editors has been to open the columns of the QUARTERLY to "articles upon any and every division of the art or craft of collecting books, from black letter missals to the modern first edition."

The QUARTERLY is the COLOPHON of England. While not quite up to the standard of the American publication, illustrations for example being omitted, yet its deluxe edition, publication of which was, unfortunately, owing to the business depression, brought to a close at the end of 1932, is eminently satisfactory to the bookman as a general publication devoted to the interests of all who concern themselves with the study of books.

BOOKS ABOUT BOOKS

Book-Lore

> BOOK-LORE, A monthly magazine devoted to old time literature, vols. 1-6, December 1884-November 1887. 8vo, illustrated. London, 1885-1887.
>
> $6.50

In December 1884 THE BIBLIOGRAPHER was incorporated with this periodical. No more were published. In December 1887 BOOK-LORE was incorporated with THE BOOKMAN.

Book-Lover's Almanac, The

> THE BOOK-LOVER'S ALMANAC. With articles by many distinguished collectors, including William Loring Andrews, Beverly Chew, W. Irving May, Eugene Field, Octave Uzanne, Charles D. Allen, H. P. Du Bois, William Matthews, Theodore L. De Vinne, O. A. Bierstadt, W. J. Linton, Henry Houssaye, S. P. Avery, etc. Illustrated with a large number of etchings, colored plates, facsimiles, etc., 5 vols., 12 mo, decorated paper wrappers, uncut. New York, 1893-97.
>
> $15.00

For each of the four years of publication both a trade and a limited edition were published. The regular editions consisted of 450 copies on Van Gelden paper and they usually sell today for about $2.50 each. The limited editions were of 100 copies on Japan paper and now bring about $4.50.

These little booklets are filled with entertaining essays and anecdotes of interest to the bookman. Complete sets in both the limited and the regular edition are now scarce. They are worthy of the collector's shelves.

Book-Lover's Library, The

> THE BOOK-LOVER'S LIBRARY, Edited by Henry B. Wheatley. 26 vols., half polished calf extra, t.e.g. London' 1886.
>
> $65.00

This is an interesting collection of book lore by such well known authors and authorities as the following:

Hazlitt, W. Carew   OLD COOKERY BOOKS AND ANCIENT CUISINE, 1886
Gomme, G. L.   THE LITERATURE OF LOCAL INSTITUTIONS, 1886

THE BIO-BIBLIOGRAPHY

Wheatley, H. B.	HOW TO FORM A LIBRARY, 1896
Wheatley, H. B.	THE DEDICATION OF BOOKS, 1897
Wheatley, H. B.	HOW TO CATALOGUE A LIBRARY, 1889
Smith, Edward	FOREIGN VISITORS TO ENGLAND AND WHAT THEY HAVE THOUGHT OF US, 1889
Pendleton, John	NEWSPAPER REPORTING IN OLDEN TIME AND TODAY, 1890
Hazlitt, W. Carew	STUDIES IN JOCULAR LITERATURE, 1890
Wheatley, Leonard A.	THE STORY OF THE 'IMITATIO CHRISTI,' 1891
Farrar, James Anson	BOOKS CONDEMNED TO BE BURNT, 1892
Wheatley, H. B.	LITERARY BLUNDERS, A CHAPTER IN THE HISTORY OF HUMAN ERROR, 1893
White, Gleeson	BOOK-SONG, 1893
Marston, R. B.	WALTON AND SOME EARLIER WRITERS ON FISH AND FISHING, 1894
Ditchfield, P. H.	BOOKS FATAL TO THEIR AUTHORS, 1895
Roberts, W.	BOOK-VERSE, 1896
Matthew, James E.	THE LITERATURE OF MUSIC, 1896
Lawless, John	BOOK AUCTIONS IN ENGLAND (1676-1700), 1898
Kitton, Frederic G.	THE NOVELS OF CHARLES DICKENS, A BIBLIOGRAPHY AND SKETCH, 1900
Saunders	THE STORY OF SOME FAMOUS BOOKS, 1888
Hazlitt, W. Carew	GLEANINGS IN OLD GARDEN LITERATURE
Blades	BOOKS IN CHAINS, 1892
Blades	MODERN METHODS OF ILLUSTRATING BOOKS, 1890
Blades	THE ENEMIES OF BOOKS, 1888
Clouston	THE BOOK OF NOODLES, 1888
Wheatley, H. B.	HOW TO MAKE AN INDEX, 1902

The writer has bought individual volumes of the ordinary edition, bound in green cloth, at prices varying from seventy-five cents to three dollars. The two items by Kitton, THE NOVELS OF CHARLES DICKENS and THE MINOR WRITINGS OF CHARLES DICKENS are the most valuable of the series.

Books about Books

BOOKS ABOUT BOOKS, edited by A. W. Pollard, comprising EARLY PRINTED BOOKS by E. Gordon Duff, EARLY ILLUSTRATED BOOKS by A. W. Pollard, BOOKS IN MANUSCRIPT by Falconer Madam, BOOKPLATES by W. J. Hardy, THE GREAT BOOK-COLLECTORS by C. I. and M. A. Elton, BOOK-BINDING by H. P. Horne. 6 vols., tall 8vo, plates and

> facsimiles, large paper, limited to 150 copies on Dutch handmade paper, uncut, half parchment. London, 1893.
> $70.00
>
> Another set. 8vo, red buckram, uncut, gold ornament and title. London, 1893.
> $35.00
>
> Another set. 8vo, brown cloth, paper label. Second edition. London, 1920.
> $12.00

This series of books represents a classic set in the literature of book collecting and might well constitute the keystone of a collection of books about books. The authors of the various volumes are authorities in their respective fields and their names are well known to all bookmen.

The series has gone through several reprints and is by no means scarce, although of the large paper limited edition the writer has seen a copy advertised for sale only once in this country.

Book Prices Current

> BOOK PRICES CURRENT, Being a Record of the Prices at which Books Have Been Sold at Auction, the Titles and Descriptions in Full, the Names of the Purchasers, etc. 8vo, cloth. London, 1887.
> $15.00

First compiled in 1887 by J. H. Slater, that prolific writer of books about books, and published by Elliot Stock of London. These volumes form another valuable record of auction prices. It must be understood, however, that no published record of auction prices contain a record of all items sold in any one year. As an example of this, during the first decade of the existence of BOOK PRICES CURRENT more than 47,000 lots of books were sold at auction. Only 6,594 or, roughly, one out of seven were recorded. Naturally, the editor of any auction record tries not to omit any really important item and while, therefore, a price record of all books sold at auction will not be found, the more important books are listed and usually nearly every author whose works have sold in any one year is represented by at least one or two price quotations.

Book Sales

> BOOK SALES of 1895-1897, A Record of the Most Important Books Sold at Auction and the Prices Realized, with Notes, Index, etc., Compiled by Temple Scott. 3 vols., thick 8vo, cloth, gilt top. London, 1895-99.
> $7.50

This three volume record of English book auction prices naturally duplicates many of the items listed in BOOK PRICES CURRENT and in BOOK AUCTION RECORDS, yet the compiler, Temple Scott, has a distinct method of his own. His descriptions, while taken from current dealers' catalogues of the time are complete and his introductions in each volume are well worth reading. The volumes are substantially bound in green cloth. The first volume was published by P. Cochran, the second and third by George Bell and Son. For the first volume, Henry Stevens, Son and Stiles were the American agents while the Macmillan Company fulfilled the function for the other two volumes.

Boutwell, H. S. (-1931)

> FIRST EDITIONS OF TO-DAY AND HOW TO TELL THEM. 12 mo, cloth. London, 1928.
> $1.50

The greater portion of this book consists of a series of detailed statements, secured presumably through circularizing publishers, as to the signs or their absence by which the first editions of certain modern authors might be identified. This is a handy little volume of sixty-four pages of interest to the collector of English firsts.

Bresford, James

> BIBLIOSOPHIA: OR BOOK-WISDOM, Containing Some Account of the Pride, Pleasure and Privileges of that Glorious Vocation, Book Collecting, by an Aspirant; The Twelve Labours of an Editor, separately Pitted Against those of Hercules. 8vo, orig. boards, uncut. First edition, London, 1810.
> $15.00

Published a year after the Rev. Thomas F. Dibdin's BIBLIOMANIA OR BOOK MADNESS appeared, the first of the two "pieces" embraced in the somewhat elaborate

BOOKS ABOUT BOOKS

title, contains, as the advertisement in the fore part of the book states, "a feeling Remonstrance against the prose work, lately published by the Reverend T. F. D." A good deal of satire was written back in the day of this little publication and the collector of Dibdin's time undoubtedly enjoyed the caricature of his hobby which, to a great extent, played a lively part in keeping the game alive.

Very little satire of this type is written today, perhaps because publishers and dealers do not encourage it. There did appear, however, in Franklin P. Adams' column, "The Conning Tower" in the World for November 19, 1928, the following report of a conversation between two ardent bibliophiles:

"I'm glad to see you. You know, there are so few people in this world who really love and cherish old books."

"There are certainly not many who appreciate the thrill that comes from possessing a rare old volume. Have you come across any interesting incunabula lately?"

"No, but I've had some luck with some Americana. The other day I got hold of Stribble's A JOURNEY ALONG THE SLAPANACKAMAW RIVER, ITS TRIBUTARIES AND NEIGHBORING CREEKS IN APRIL 1763 AND JUNE 1766. Paid seventeen for it, and sold it to Rosencrantz for twenty-six."

"I got thirty-five for Poomley's A RECORD OF RAIN AND SNOWFALL IN SOUTHEASTERN VERMONT AND NORTHWESTERN NEW HAMPSHIRE IN 1795. I hated to part with it."

"I could kick myself for letting old Wilgus have REFLECTIONS AND COMMENTARIES ON THE GROWTH AND CULTIVATION OF ROOTABAGA AND KINDRED VEGETABLES AMONG THE INDIANS OF POOTANAGRA COUNTY, PENNSYLVANIA, IN 1787. I let it go at forty and now I hear it's listed at sixty-two."

"It's best to keep an old volume and treasure it. As time passes you find that it becomes more and more precious to you."

"Quite true. I wouldn't part with my copy of THE MANUFACTURE AND DISTRIBUTION OF WHIPSOCKETS IN ITS RELATION TO A BILL PROHIBITING FISHING ON THE SABBATH INTRODUCED BY LEMUEL SYLVESTER FINNING INTO THE CONNECTICUT LEGISLATURE IN 1804 AND PASSED IN 1807."

"I'll give you $25, and my copy of Lubhullins' THE PREVALENCE OF GLANDERS AMONG THE HORSES OF CERTAIN PORTIONS OF MASSACHUSETTS LYING SOUTH AND WEST OF BOSTON IN THE SPRING OF 1801 for it."

"We-ell, let's go to lunch and talk it over."

"Let's. I'm just aching for some book chat."
"Same here. There's something about old books that gets you."
"There certainly is. Now as I was saying, I'll give you . . ."

Brewer, Luther A. (1858-   )

> THE LOVE OF BOOKS, with a reprint of Leigh Hunt's essay on "My Books." 8vo, boards, parchment back. One of 300 copies, privately printed, Cedar Rapids, Christmas, 1923.
>
> $6.00

A brief description of this book is included in these pages not because of any particular aid or interest that the volume has for the average collector, except that by chance he be an enthusiast of Hunt as is Mr. Brewer, but simply because THE LOVE OF BOOKS is an excellent example of the sincerity with which most collectors follow their hobby. The book has, as well, a high standard of typographic excellence as have so many other privately printed books which, from time to time, come from the pens of earnest collectors. These collector-author-publishers, writing for their own entertainment and that of their friends, let no thought of monetary reward cloud their minds or disturb their pleasure in the production of their little volumes.

Mr. Brewer brought together during his lifetime one of the finest Leigh Hunt collections in America. In other small volumes he tells of the successes and failures incurred in his collecting activities, describes some of his Hunt items and reproduces various letters to Keats, Shelley, Byron, and other of Hunt's contemporaries.

This is one of a series of eight books in which Mr. Brewer records his studies on Leigh Hunt. All of these books were privately printed by Mr. Brewer at the Torch Press in Cedar Rapids, Iowa. From this press have also come many of the attractive catalogues issued by large Eastern dealers.

Luther Brewer was that rare combination of collector, printer and bibliographer. He has made a lasting contribution to the literature of book collecting and bibliography. This is particularly true of his bibliography of Hunt entitled MY LEIGH HUNT LIBRARY, which had the distinction of being recorded in the Bulletin of the Boston Public Library as "one of the finest works of its kind."

Among the separate publications written and published by Mr. Brewer dealing with Hunt and his associates are the following:

BOOKS ABOUT BOOKS

AROUND THE LIBRARY TABLE, an Evening with Leigh Hunt, 1920. With two facsimiles of two letters from Hunt to Severn.

LEIGH HUNT'S ROBIN HOOD, 1921. Reprint of the entire poem with facsimiles of portions of original draft.

STEVENSON'S PERFECT VIRTUES as exemplified by Leigh Hunt, 1922.

THE LOVE OF BOOKS, 1923. With a reprint of Leigh Hunt's Essays on "My Books."

SOME LAMB AND BROWNING LETTERS to Leigh Hunt, 1924. With facsimiles of four letters from Lamb to Hunt, one from Hunt to Mrs. Shelley, one from Hunt to Browning and one from Browning to Hunt.

WANDERINGS IN LONDON, 1925.

MARGINALIA, 1926.

Browne, Irving (1835-1899)

IN THE TRACK OF THE BOOKWORM, Thoughts, Fancies, and Gentle Gibes on Collecting and Collectors, by One of Them. Limited to 590 copies signed by the author. 8vo, boards, uncut. East Aurora, 1897.

$7.50

Browne has incorporated in the above volume a series of amusing book ballads with authoritative and instructive chapters on Collecting, Bindings, Book-Plates, Book-Sellers and other subjects dear to every collector. The pages are decorated with red ornamental paragraph letters and marginal titles. The book is a good example of Roycroft printing and contains a great deal of useful information. It is easy to read and will contribute greatly to one's "booklore."

BALLADS OF A BOOK-WORM, Being a Rhythmic Record of Thoughts, Fancies and Adventures of Collecting, East Aurora, 1899, which appeared in a hand illuminated edition of 850 copies and is worth today $1.50, is by the same author.

Burton, John Hill (1809-1881)

THE BOOK-HUNTER. Large paper, small square 4to, red cloth, brown morocco back, gilt, uncut, limited to 25 copies. First edition, Edinburgh, 1863.

$35.00

THE BIO-BIBLIOGRAPHY

THE BOOK-HUNTER, A New Edition with a Memoir of the Author. Thick 4to, frontispiece of the author and four other illustrations, blue cloth, gilt, gold ornament in center, uncut, large paper, limited to 1000 copies. Second edition, Edinburgh, 1882.
$10.00

In addition to the above described scarce first edition, there have been numerous reprints in England and America. The so-called best or second edition was also printed on large paper but in an edition of 1000 copies and in an entirely different format. Burton, an advocate by profession, was appointed Secretary to the Prison Board in 1854 and in 1867 became Royal Historiographer of Scotland. With the exception of this book, however, his writings are little remembered. Upon publication it became and remains a standard work.

The general Table of Contents is descriptive of the scope and character of the book. Divided into four parts it includes: The Book-Hunter. Part I—His Nature; Part II—His Functions; Part III—His Club; Part IV—Book-Club Literature. The various parts are subdivided into numerous chapters. The first edition is not indexed, nor is it illustrated as is the second edition, which also has a good index. The second edition was printed after Burton's death, the Memoir being by his widow.

From early manhood, Burton was a book-collector. His library, which he catalogued and sold in 1880, comprised some ten thousand volumes. Incidentally, he was disappointed in the proceeds of its sale.

Briggs, Morris (1890-   )

BUYING AND SELLING RARE BOOKS. 8vo, boards. New York, 1927.
$3.50

This slim little volume strikes a new note among books about books. It was written by a Chicago rare book dealer as a guide for others and particularly for young dealers. The contents which were revised for publication in book form appeared originally in THE PUBLISHERS' WEEKLY, as a series of articles on "Building a Rare Book Department." Even though intended principally as a text book for the trade, a considerable amount of useful information for the collector lies within its covers. This book makes it possible for the general reader as well to gain some insight into the methods employed in carrying on a rare book business.

BOOKS ABOUT BOOKS

Carter, John (1905-   )

BINDING VARIANTS IN ENGLISH PUBLISHING, 1820-1900, Bibliographical Series No. 6. 8vo, marbled boards, vellum back. Constable, London; Long and Smith, 16 collotype plates, New York, 1933.

$6.50

Students of the history of book structure and all collectors of nineteenth century first editions in their original condition will be particularly interested in this book for it deals in a scientific way with a point in bibliography, not clearly explained in the past but which is of vast importance to the meticulous collector. The first section of BINDING VARIANTS outlines the general historical and practical principles applicable to the problems of binding variants; while the second section includes a detailed analysis of a hundred books, all of interest to the collector and all possessing two or more bindings not hitherto adequately discussed. In general the book comprises a detailed and much needed treatise, bibliographically sound and readable, on the development of publisher's binding since the introduction of cloth. The work is really a supplement of Michael Sadler's THE EVOLUTION OF PUBLISHER'S BINDING STYLES (No. 1 of the Bibliographical Series). It is attractively printed and includes a number of interesting illustrations.

Carter, John and Graham Pollard

AN ENQUIRY INTO THE NATURE OF CERTAIN NINETEENTH CENTURY PAMPHLETS. Four plates, 8vo, cloth, t.e.g. London and New York, 1934.

$6.00

The advent of this book of Messrs. Carter and Pollard has undoubtedly caused more written and oral comment by collectors and dealers in this country and in England than any previously published book about books. In fact, it comes close to being the most sensational book with reference to the collecting and authenticity of English first editions that has ever been written. The publisher's own description of the book is of such importance that it is reproduced in full.

"This book is a fully documented exposure of a group of more than fifty 'first editions' of such eminent authors as Wordsworth, Tennyson, Dickens, Thackeray, the Brownings, Swinburne, George Eliot, William Morris, R. L.

Stevenson and Rudyard Kipling. These books are mostly of the 'privately printed' or 'pre-first' pamphlet. They appear in all the standard bibliographies and have been generally accepted for upwards of thirty years. Many of them command considerable prices in the market.

"In the light of the evidence assembled here, more than thirty of them are shown to be forgeries and the status of the remainder is open to considerable suspicion.

"The exposure of the real character of these books introduces scientific methods which have never before been applied to bibliographical problems of this period. The paper has been analysed under the microscope and its evidence assessed in the light of some original research into the history of paper manufacture. The peculiarities of type have been traced to the printer. The involved story of the establishment of these books in the bibliographies and the rare book market is patiently unravelled.

"These revelations will entail considerable revision among the bibliographies of the authors concerned, and cannot fail to have serious repercussions on the market price both of the forgeries themselves and of the first editions which they have supplanted. The whole story of suspicion, detection and proof gives a vivid picture of a fraud which, for its extent and for the extraordinary skill of its conception and execution, is without a parallel in the history of bibliography and book collecting."

The exposure of these forgeries, and it seems evident from the case Carter and Pollard have worked up that little doubt can exist but that the nineteenth century items mentioned were spurious, brought no word of explanation from their late champion and distributor, Thomas J. Wise, long known as one of the foremost English collectors and bibliographers. The entire story presents a fascinating riddle which collectors and dealers trust before long will be satisfactorily answered.

Chapman, R. W. (1881-   )

CANCELS. With 11 facsimiles in collotype and a folding plate concerned with watermarks. 8vo, marbled boards, vellum back, colored top, uncut, limited to 500 copies. First edition, London and New York, 1930.
$8.00

This is a book of permanent value to the student of book structure containing a brilliant study of one of the most perplexing of all bibliographical problems. It is of particular importance as a reference work to collectors of eighteenth century books.

Clark, John W. (1833-1910)

>THE CARE OF BOOKS, An Essay on the Development of Libraries and their Fittings, from the Earliest Times to the End of the Eighteenth Century. Royal 8vo, black cloth, gilt title, t.e.g., 156 illustrations. Cambridge, England, 1901.
>
>$10.00

Written by a former Fellow of Trinity College who was also a Sandars Reader in Bibliography before the University of Cambridge and Registrar of the University, this is truly a great book. In this history of libraries from the earliest times, the author has carefully traced the methods adopted in different ages and countries to preserve, use and make accessible to others the objects, of whatever material, upon which man has recorded his thoughts.

THE CARE OF BOOKS deals with an extremely wide and interesting subject. It is a valuable reference and will give the bookman a better understanding of old libraries than any other publication that has come to the attention of the writer. The many photographic illustrations are wonderfully clear and are supplemented by numerous pen and ink sketches and line drawings. The book is well indexed and highly recommended.

Clements, William L. (1861-1934)

>THE WILLIAM L. CLEMENTS LIBRARY OF AMERICANA. 8vo, boards, black cloth back, paper label. Cambridge, Massachusetts, 1923.
>
>$3.00

For the most part, book collectors are an unappreciated group. Usually to obtain recognition a collector must at his death possess a library of no mean proportions. Even then, if his books were sold at auction, he would quickly be forgotten. One of the surest ways to immortality for the collector, provided he is wealthy enough, is to endow his collection in order that it may be properly housed, cared for, added to and made available throughout future generations to students and other collectors.

An example of one such collection adequately housed and provided for during the owner's lifetime is the William L. Clement's Library of Americana at Ann Arbor, Michigan. The aim and purpose of this library is well described in the above volume. Mr. Randolph G. Adams, the librarian, has issued an invaluable series of catalogues and bulletins describing many of the scarce items deposited by Mr. Clements in this library. Furthermore, it is the sincere desire of the founder himself to help others who are interested in books or who have some particularly difficult bit of research work in hand. If you ever visit Ann Arbor and find the main entrance to this library locked, just go around to the side door where a gentle knock will bring Mr. Adams or one of his capable assistants to let you in. The William L. Clements Library is open even after hours to those who have need of its facilities.

Students and historians will long recognize the great debt owed to Mr. Clements for a collection that will make it necessary for future historians to make a pilgrimage to Ann Arbor rather than to any other library in the country. The University of Michigan should indeed be grateful to him.

The son of a steel manufacturer, William L. Clements provides one of the rare instances of a son successfully taking over and expanding his father's business. He retired a wealthy man in 1924. In 1923 he presented to the University of Michigan his accumulated books and manuscripts together with the building in which they now rest. He lived for eleven years to enjoy and see appreciated the fruits of his collecting endeavors.

The library is rich in unique and valuable Americana and includes 50,000 documents of the Earl of Shelburne, British Prime Minister at the end of the American revolution; 25,000 documents and 350 handmade maps of Sir Henry Clinton comprising the actual British Headquarters Papers; 15 folio manuscript volumes of Lord Germain, British Colonial Secretary; and the official files of General Thomas Gage, British Commander-in-Chief. This is probably the most important bundle of manuscripts that ever crossed the Atlantic. There are also in the collection Burgoyne's and Cornwallis' letters reporting surrender; Benjamin Franklin's letter refusing to compensate the Tories; Pitcairn's report of the Battle of Lexington, and a letter of Christopher Columbus describing his first voyage.

Cole, George Watson (1850-   )

A SURVEY OF THE BIBLIOGRAPHY OF ENGLISH LITERATURE, 1475-1640, with Especial Reference to the work of the Bibliographical Society of London. Vol. 23, Part II, Papers of the Bibliographical Society of America, Chicago, 1929.

$2.00

BOOKS ABOUT BOOKS

For the student of bibliography and the collector, this volume comprises one of the most practical papers ever issued by the Bibliographical Society of America and its author, through a lifetime of devotion to all aspects of the science he represents, is well qualified to write authoritatively.

Graduating from the Columbia Library School in 1888, Dr. Cole spent ten years in active public library work, after which he resigned to devote himself to bibliography. He was from 1915 to 1924 librarian of the great Henry E. Huntington collection at San Marino, California and since 1924 has been Librarian Emeritus. He has compiled a long list of library catalogues and is the author of numerous books and monographs pertaining to books and collectors.

A SURVEY OF THE BIBLIOGRAPHY OF ENGLISH LITERATURE is rich in its biographical contributions to the lives of the men who have been responsible for most of the bibliographical guides with which the collector is, or should be, familiar. All the old bookmen as well as some of the new authorities are represented in impressive array—Bohn, Collier, Lowndes, Dibdin, Blades, Duff, Hazlitt, DeRicci, Huth, Locker-Lamson, Madam, Rylands, and Huntington— to mention a few who are linked inseparably, as they should be, with their bibliographical contributions.

In five chapters, one of which is an introduction outlining the scope and value of the work, the reader is given a survey of bibliographical literature, a description of the endeavors of private book collectors and institutions, together with specimen pages of comment and specimens to illustrate the gradual development of descriptive bibliography and style.

If possible, all of the papers of the Bibliographical Societies of London and America should be on the shelves of the collector. This is a rather large order, however, and, except in instances where funds need not be considered, should not be taken seriously by the average collector, unless he is particularly interested in books about books. This particular number of the papers, however, is well worth including in one's library, for its contents are far from being of a technical nature.

Cole, George Watson (1850-   )

BIBLIOGRAPHICAL PITFALLS—LINKED BOOKS, Reprinted for private distribution from Papers of the Bibliographical Society of America. Vol. 18, parts 1, 2; 19 pp., Chicago, 1926.

$5.00

THE BIO-BIBLIOGRAPHY

This is a technical monograph upon one phase of the science of bibliography. The paper should appear in any collection of books about books, yet does not concern most collectors. Doctor Cole describes certain volumes that have appeared with a general title page, register and pagination but which have separate title pages and in some cases may have appeared as separate publications. A method is suggested by the author for dealing with this class of books and his monograph contains many helpful suggestions. The essay is a reprint, having originally appeared in the Papers of the Bibliographical Society of America.

Cole, George Watson (1850-   )

BIBLIOGRAPHICAL GHOSTS. Reprinted from the Papers of the Bibliographical Society of America. Vol. 13, Part 2, 28 pp. 8vo, wrappers. One of 100 copies. Chicago, 1920.

$2.00

The "ghosts" are editions appearing in bibliographies, but which never existed.

Collier, J. Payne (1789-1883)

RARE ENGLISH BOOKS. Tall 8vo., 4 vols., red cloth, one of 75 copies. New York, 1866.

$30.00

First Edition, 8vo., roxburgh, 2 vols. Joseph Lilly, London, 1865.

$40.00

Comprising a bibliography of the rarest books in the English language alphabetically arranged and treating especially of Elizabethan and early Stuart literature, this work has remained a standard reference. Each item described is supplemented with a lengthy bibliographical and literary note.

Colophon, The

THE COLOPHON. 4 vols., 4to, decorative boards, fore and lower edges uncut, illustrations and facsimiles, limited to 2000 copies. Volume I, Parts 1-4, New York, Feb., May, Sept., and Dec., 1930.

$45.00

BOOKS ABOUT BOOKS

Volume II, Parts 5-8. Limited to 3000 copies. New York, March, June, Sept. and Dec., 1931.
$15.00

Volume III, Parts 9-12. Limited to 3000 copies. New York, Feb., May, Sept., and Dec., 1932.
$15.00

Volume IV, Parts 13-16. Limited to 2500 copies. New York, Feb., June, Oct., March, 1933-34.
$15.00

Volume V, Parts 17-20. Limited to 1700 copies. New York, June, Sept., Dec., March, 1934-35.
$15.00

INDEX, Original Series, THE COLOPHON, with A History of the Quarterly by John T. Winterich, and A Listing of Types and Papers by Peter Beilenson. 8vo, blue cloth, gilt. New York, 1935.
$2.60

THE COLOPHON, as a collector's journal published in America, out-ranks anything heretofore attempted along this line. Its nearest competitor is the limited edition of THE BOOK COLLECTOR'S QUARTERLY published by the First Edition Club of London, which, in spite of its fine typography, binding and character of contents, remains unillustrated.

Begun in 1929, the quarterly issues of THE COLOPHON, have been eagerly sought by collectors, the first four issues now bringing three to four times their original price. Splendid articles by such authors and writers on bookish subjects as H. L. Mencken, Sherwood Anderson, Christopher Morley, William McFee, Theodore Dreiser, James Branch Cabell, Willa Cather, William A. Kettredge, Oscar Lewis, Frederick W. Goudy, James Laver, W. A. Rogers, Seymour DeRicci, Michael Sadlier, and Lillian Gary whose topics include a discussion of first editions, incunabula, bibliography, association books, manuscripts and Americana, are to be found within the covers of this splendid publication.

Strange as it may seem, though its birth occurred at perhaps the height of the limited edition craze, THE COLOPHON was not begun as a money-making venture. This fact may account in a large measure for its character and success. Its original production and publication were made possible by the generosity of a bibliophile who remains anonymous.

The original list of contributing editors as published in volume one, include the following names, all well known in the bookman's and collector's world: Elmer Adler, Thomas Beer, Pierce Butler, W. A. Dwiggins, John G. Eckel, Burton Emmett, Frederick W. Goudy, Ruth S. Granniss, Belle D. Costa Greene, David Hunter, William M. Ivins, Jr., Henry W. Kent, Rockwell Kent, Christopher Morley, Verst Orton, Bruce Rogers, Carl P. Rollins, George H. Sargent, Gilbert M. Troxell, D. B. Updike, George P. Winship and John T. Winterich. They well deserve some mention on this page and would that it were within the writer's ability to give them more worthy credit for the excellent work they have done. While in the beginning THE COLOPHON enjoyed a fund for expenses, it now depends entirely on subscribers for support. The publication has won its way to the hearts of book collectors and lovers of fine printing. Its future seems assured.

An index to a publication of the character of THE COLOPHON is a most necessary tool and its preparation, hardly an easy task for the editors, brought the first series of THE COLOPHON to a well rounded close. Mr. Winterich's essay on the history of the Quarterly is a most interesting, complete and carefully written account of the many problems that were met in originating and carrying on this fascinating journal. Mr. Beilenson contributes a most satisfactory description and check list of the type faces and various papers used in its printing.

Colophon, The (New Series)

THE COLOPHON, A Quarterly for Bookmen. 8vo, decorative boards, illustrated. Vol. I, Numbers I-IV, New York, 1935-36.
$10.00
Volume II, Numbers I- — New York, 1936- —
$6.00

The New Series of THE COLOPHON continues in much the same vein the work of the original issue. The subscription cost has been reduced, however, from fifteen dollars a year to six dollars. The format has been changed considerably and the illustrations are not as numerous nor as elaborate. However, the text and general character of the articles have suffered no let down as a result of the reduction in size and price of THE COLOPHON. In fact, the new volumes are of a most convenient size and many readers believe them of even greater practical value than were the earlier volumes.

BOOKS ABOUT BOOKS

Courtney, William P. (1845-1913)

> A REGISTER OF NATIONAL BIBLIOGRAPHY, with a Selection of the Chief Bibliographical Books and Articles Printed in Other Countries. 3 vols. London, 1905-12.
> $10.00

A bibliography of bibliography is always welcomed by the collector as a valuable working tool. This particular work does not give a select list of books on any given subject but it does instruct the reader where to find such lists already in print. The book is, in effect, a source of information on practically every subject upon which published writings exist. One can understand, after perusing only a few of the twenty-one thousand odd entries, the extent of Mr. Courtney's achievement. It is not surprising to know that he contemplated the work for fully twenty years and was actively occupied with the aid of several assistants for four years in its compilation. Mr. Courtney rightly deserves a high place among bookmen for his contribution to bibliography, and the book itself belongs on the shelves of every collector's working library.

Crummer, LeRoy (1872-1934)

> A CATALOGUE OF MANUSCRIPTS AND MEDICAL BOOKS PRINTED BEFORE 1640. 8vo, 95 pp., yellow cloth, limited to 100 copies. Privately printed, Omaha, 1928.
> $10.00

Physicians and surgeons have long constituted a large percentage of book collectors. It is with considerable pleasure in recognition of this fact that mention is here made of the catalogue of a portion of the collection of medical books made by Dr. LeRoy Crummer. The publication of this volume was really the work of Mrs. Crummer, who, all unknown to her husband, selected from his notes sufficient material to make up the little book. She has written an able foreword in which she supports her contention that the collecting of medical books is an absorbing and worthy pursuit.

Medical books are occupying the attention of collectors more than ever before and the buyers of these items are by no means confined to members of the profession. This CATALOGUE of the Crummers, for they were collaborators in collecting, is a valuable bibliographical help to anyone interested in the field.

It describes a library of some 386 volumes unusual in its extent and variety.

George H. Sargent said of this work, "the CATALOGUE serves its purpose, which is to describe each book so that it will not be confounded with some other book or some other edition." He also reminds one that Mrs. Crummer, in compiling the list, "points out that if one is interested in early printing, an example of the work of practically every great printing establishment for two hundred years after the invention of printing may be found in a medical collection."

Curle, Richard (1883-   )

> COLLECTING AMERICAN FIRST EDITIONS, Its Pitfalls and Pleasures. 51 plates of title pages and bindings. 8vo., full black cloth, gilt top, paper labels, uncut. One of 1050 copies signed by the author. Indianapolis, 1930.
> $12.50

This is a valuable work for the collector. Mr. Curle deals with the great names in American literature and authoritatively sets forth in considerable detail the ordinary as well as the obscure points which distinguish the early editions of American authors from Washington Irving to Mark Twain. The detection of forged copies is likewise covered.

Currie, Barton (1878-   )

> FISHERS OF BOOKS. 8vo., cloth paper label, numerous illustrations. Boston, 1931.
> $4.00
> Limited edition, one of 365 signed copies, 2 vols., 8vo., boards. Boston, 1931.
> $12.50

For some years Mr. Currie stuck to his desk succeeding Edward Bok as editor of the Ladies Home Journal. It was, undoubtedly, a profitable editorship, for Mr. Currie was able to purchase an extraordinary variety of first editions and manuscripts which he enthusiastically describes in this book. Consisting, on the whole, in a narrative of the author's experiences, the book is written in pleasant style but is not without errors. Considering the range covered, however, this is not to be wondered at. Some of the prices mentioned have since proved sad reading to many of Mr. Currie's contemporaries, but this is likewise true of any work that covers the subject of book collecting during the late period of fantastic prices.

Davenport, Cyril (1848-   )

BY-WAYS AMONG ENGLISH BOOKS. 8vo, boards. London, 1926.

$3.00

This is a splendid little book with seventy-seven drawings and other illustrations dealing with collectors and collecting. It contains a great deal of interesting material on curious books. Printed, illustrated, miniature, embroidered and horn books are among those described. The amateur collector will find it easy reading and filled with useful information. Mr. Davenport, at one time with the British Museum, is an English bibliophile of note.

De Bury, Richard (1287-1345)

THE PHILOBIBLON or The Love of Books, newly translated by E. C. Thomas. Frontispiece, square 12mo, boards, 1913.

$1.25

The first true translation, as it is known today, of THE PHILOBIBLON was made by Thomas James in 1599 and seems to be quite rare. Three years after completing this work, he became the first Bodleian librarian, yet, in spite of his bibliographical knowledge, he knew only one of the two translations which preceded his own.

THE PHILOBIBLON was first printed in Cologne in 1473, and numerous editions followed until 1888 when the translation by Mr. E. C. Thomas was issued by Kegan, Paul, French and Company of London. This edition was reproduced by the De LaMore Press in the form described above and is an excellent reading copy of this first treatise on book collecting that has come down to us from the Middle Ages.

Book collecting really began with Richard de Bury, an Oxford student and subsequently tutor of the Prince who later became Edward III. De Bury held many offices upon the accession of Edward. Among others, he was ambassador to Rome, which post undoubtedly contributed largely to his passion for assembling books. He was the forerunner of all modern collectors, but none since has succumbed in greater degree to the disease, bibliomania. Until his death at fifty-eight he literally lived among his books. Each of his residences contained what was for his time an immense number of books. In fact, he probably owned more books than all the rest of his fellow English bishops together.

The interest for the collector in De Bury begins with his third chapter in which he discusses so ably the prices of books. As a matter of satisfaction and justification for the reader whose conscience may be troubling him over recent purchases, it is worth while to record here a portion of the excuse De Bury gives for paying the bills that collectors incur. While the statement may not hold water when repeated to a long suffering wife, yet it is warranted to make the heart of even the most parsimonious collector beat a bit faster. He says, ". . . no dearness of price ought to hinder a man from the buying of books if he has the money that is demanded for them unless it be to withstand the malice of the seller or to await a more favorable opportunity for buying. For if it is wisdom only that makes the price of books, which is an infinite treasure to mankind, and if the value of books is unspeakable as the premises show, how shall the bargain be shown to be dear where an infinite good is being sought? Wherefore, that books are to be gladly bought and willingly sold, Solomon, the sum of man, exhorts us in the Proverb, 'Buy the trust and sell not the wisdom.'"

Rather dull and long winded on the whole, De Bury is worth reading if only for the amusing way in which he outlines the methods by which so many volumes, costing him not a penny, came into his possession. He speaks for "due propriety in the custody of books," and his descriptions of the ways in which harm may come to a book are outranked only by Sinclair Lewis with his reference, in BABBITT, to the youth with the running nose who does not think of using his handkerchief "until he has dewed the book before him with ugly moisture."

deHalsalle, Henry (1872-)

TREASURE TROVE IN BOOKLAND, The Romance of Modern First Editions. 8vo., boards. First edition, London, 1931.
$2.50
THE ROMANCE OF MODERN FIRST EDITIONS. 8vo., cloth. Philadelphia, 1931.
$1.50

Covering a wide range from incunabula and black letter books down to the date of publication, the author describes various books he believes worth col-

DeRicci, Seymour (1881-   )

> A CENSUS OF CAXTONS, with frontispiece, and ten facsimiles. 4to, wrappers. Bibliographical Society, Oxford, 1909.
>
> $30.00

DeRicci's CENSUS was written by him in Paris over a period of three years and was printed in 1909 by the Oxford University Press as the twenty-fifth Illustrated Monograph of the Bibliographical Society.

This particular copy, now in the writer's library, belonged at one time to the Free Reference Library of Bath as is evidenced by the seal embossed on the brown paper wrapper, as well as by the ascension number, classification and location marks which some industrious cataloguer at one time carefully handlettered in ink. One might indeed speculate on the circumstances surrounding the appearance of this one-time library copy among the offerings of a Liverpool bookseller and its subsequent resting place on the shelves of a collector in America.

DeRicci's contribution to the bibliographical knowledge of Caxton's work is attractively printed on handmade, uncut paper. The margins are unusually wide. It is of little practical use to the ordinary collector who, as a rule, is not in the market for Caxton's. It is only the occasional collector of means who, in this day, can buy a Caxton and thus have need for the descriptive material which DeRicci has compiled. Furthermore, nearly all known Caxtons are now safely ensconced in the great libraries of the world, as a perusal of DeRicci's catalogue will indicate. As a reference work, however, the volume is of value to librarians and those engaged in research, for it contains all of William Blake's admirable data on Caxton as well as an immense amount of original material which DeRicci was successful in amassing with the aid of a long list of associates, collectors and librarians.

Entirely regardless of the current usefulness of a bibliography of this type, the volume as a work of DeRicci's should be owned by every collector and student of the printed book who can afford to purchase a copy. DeRicci as a writer of books about books is well known and no bookman's library could approach completeness without all of his books on its shelves.

DeRicci, Seymour (1881-   )

THE BOOK COLLECTOR'S GUIDE, a Practical Handbook of British and American Bibliography. Limited to 1100 copies, 8vo, cloth, 649 pp. Rosenbach Company, Philadelphia, 1921.

$10.00

While the prices quoted in this volume are out of date, yet it is still a very interesting and practical bibliographical guide for the dealer and collector to the prices of several thousand books which have been most in demand during the last twenty years. It is becoming exceedingly hard to pick up a copy, as it is an item which is in demand—being rightly catalogued as "scarce" when offered for sale by dealers.

At the time of publication THE BOOK-COLLECTOR'S GUIDE was one of the most ambitious general bibliographies since Lowndes. Its essential purpose was to be a dictionary of rare books and to condense much essential reference material.

In addition to the above edition, which was published at $10.00, thirty copies were printed on large paper and sold at $40.00.

DeRicci, Seymour (1881-   )

ENGLISH COLLECTORS OF BOOKS AND MANUSCRIPTS (1530-1930) and Their Marks of Ownership. 8vo, original cloth, gilt. London, 1930.

$5.00

Comprising the Saunders Lectures for 1929-1930, this book is a study of the marks of ownership used by English collectors. It includes details both of modern private libraries and of those which have, in times past, been dispersed. Booklovers are always enthusiastic over anything from the pen of DeRicci. He is famous throughout the world for his knowledge of rare books and collectors. His research contributions to the literature of bibliography have maintained a high standard of scholarly accuracy and usefulness. This particular volume is no exception, for much of the information given about recent changes in ownership up to the year of its publication is not found elsewhere in print.

BOOKS ABOUT BOOKS

De Vinne, Theodore Low (1824-1914)

THE INVENTION OF PRINTING, A Collection of Facts and Opinions Descriptive of Early Prints and Playing Cards, the Block Books of the Fifteenth Century, the Legends of Lourens Janszoon Coster and the Work of John Gutenburg. Numerous facsimiles of early types and woodcuts. Large 4to, half morocco. New York, 1878.
$50.00

TITLE PAGES AS SEEN BY A PRINTER, Numerous Illustrations in Facsimile and Some Observations on the Early and Recent Printing of Books. 8vo, half morocco, one of 325 copies. Grolier Club, New York, 1901.
$40.00

NOTABLE PRINTERS OF ITALY DURING THE FIFTEENTH CENTURY. Numerous facsimiles from early editions, large 4to., half buckram. Grolier Club, New York, 1910.
$35.00

THE PRACTICE OF TYPOGRAPHY, including the following volumes, PLAIN PRINTING TYPES, 1902; CORRECT COMPOSITION, 1902; TREATISE ON TITLE PAGES, 1902; MODERN BOOK COMPOSITION, 1904. 8vo, brown cloth, morocco label, gilt, t.e.g., 4 vols. New York.
$25.00

THEODORE LOW DE VINNE PRINTER, a biographical sketch by Henry L. Bullen and tributes to De Vinne with a bibliography of his works. Privately printed on handmade paper, tall 8vo., uncut, t.e.g. The De Vinne Press, New York, 1915.
$10.00

The bibliographical sketch by Henry L. Bullen, together with the bibliography of De Vinne as printed by his press in 1915, will give the reader all the information he needs regarding one of the most famous American printers. De Vinne was the author of many books and articles on the subject of his life's work. He represented a distinct period in the development of printing in this country. A font of type bears his name which in itself is sufficient guarantee of his remembrance by typographers and bookmen.

De Vinne was an active worker as a student of typography before William Morris of the Kelmscott Press was ever heard of in connection with printing. Notes for his book, PLAIN PRINTING TYPES, were made as early as 1860. His series of books under the general title, THE PRACTICE OF TYPOGRAPHY, had much to do with cleaning up and strengthening the work of American printers just prior to the time of Morris.

Born one of six sons of a Methodist preacher, De Vinne went to work at fourteen in the office of the Newburg, New York, *Gazette* to learn the printing business. He became in time the foremost American printer of his day. Like Franklin, the most famous printer, De Vinne became wealthy. Unlike Franklin, however, De Vinne was not a publisher. He confined his efforts solely to commercial printing.

De Vinne is assured a place in the hearts of all bookmen, not only as an author and a collector of note but as one of the founders of the Grolier Club in New York. He was respectively a member of its Council, Vice President, and President.

Upon his death, his library of 1941 items was sold at auction. It was, at the time, the most important collection of books pertaining to the history and art of printing ever offered in the United States. It was, of course, primarily a working library and high prices were paid.

Dibdin, Rev. Thomas Frognall (1776-1847)

THE BIBLIOMANIA or Book Madness, Containing Some Account of the History Symptoms and Cure for this Fatal Disease. 8vo. First edition, London, 1809.

$30.00

Dibdin, whose counterpart today is quite probably a choice between Mr. A. Edward Newton, the author of THE AMENITIES OF BOOK-COLLECTING, and Mr. Holbrook Jackson, the author of THE ANATOMY OF BIBLIOMANIA, assures us in his eighty-eight page treatise that book collectors are victims of an actual disease. Poor Dibdin, though writing with a facetious tongue in his cheek, was probably much closer to the truth than he realized.

As the author of INTRODUCTION TO THE KNOWLEDGE OF RARE AND VALUABLE EDITIONS OF THE GREEK AND LATIN CLASSICS, 1802; BIBLIOSOPHIA, 1810; TYPOGRAPHICAL ANTIQUITIES, 1810-1819; BIBLIOGRAPHICAL SPENSERIANA, 1814; A BIBLIOGRAPHICAL ANTIQUARIAN AND PICTURESQUE TOUR IN FRANCE AND GERMANY, 1829; THE BIBLIOGRAPHICAL DECAMERON AND REMINISCENCES OF A LITERARY LIFE, 1836, Dibdin was the foremost writer on bibliographical topics of his day. His output has exceeded that of any subsequent author, who has sought to write about books and the many subjects that may be allied to them. While far from accurate in his observations or references, and a bit out of date at the present time, Dibdin did much at the beginning of the nineteenth century to create an active public interest in libraries and book collecting.

Born in 1776, he lived to the age of seventy-one years, enjoying great respect for his knowledge and industry, although some of his current readers may be both annoyed and amused at his verboseness. All in all, however, there is a great deal to be learned from Dibdin and the majority of his books should be in the collector's library. This is particularly true of THE BIBLIOMANIA which for the average bookman is the most interesting as well as one of the most famous of all books on collecting.

Dibdin, Thomas F. (1776-1847)

THE LIBRARY COMPANION or the Young Man's Guide and The Old Man's Comfort, in the Choice of a Library. Large thick 8vo, full calf, gilt border, red and gold label. Second edition, London, 1825.

$10.00

This book contains a great deal of curious and interesting information. Naturally, one hundred and twelve years after publication, its contents are out of date. The principles upon which Dibdin built his thesis remain, however, as true today as they did in 1825. That is the important and vital characteristic of book collecting. Read what he says in his Preface—

"From the beginning to the end I have never lost sight of what I consider to be the most material object to be gained from a publication of this nature; namely, the imparting of a moral feeling to the gratification of a literary taste. Let us consider the subject dispassionately. Great Britain is the most wealthy, and politically speaking, perhaps the most powerful kingdom upon earth. Considered in a domestic point of view, there are thousands of large and affluent families—it follows, therefore, that of the rising generation, a large proportion, inheriting a considerable property, and educated in the most accomplished manner, commence their career in life with the means and opportunities of gratifying their tastes and passions in a thousand diverse and at times contradictory pursuits. To such in particular, whether emerging from the cloisters of a college, or from the upper form of a public school, this Library Companion will be found of more consequence than may be at first imagined: for I am greatly deceived if experience does not prove that much more than half of the misery which is abroad in the world, in the higher classes of society, has arisen from the superfluous wealth. I address myself, therefore, immediately, directly, and honestly, to the young man, in whose hands such means may be deposited, to devote them to the gratification of a legitimate taste in the cultivation of Literature; and as this object cannot be accomplished without the acquisition of a Library, of greater or less extent, I venture to indulge a humble hope That This Guide, in the choice of such a Library may be found, as far as it extends, useful and accurate."

The collector interested in biblical and classical literature, in early histories of England and the principal European countries, in voyages and travels, memoirs, *belles lettres*, poetry and English drama may find in Dibdin's LIBRARY COMPANION much pertinent information that later authorities have overlooked or neglected. An excellent index of some sixty-four pages makes it easy for the reader to locate any author or subject.

D'Israeli, Issac (1766-1848)

CURIOSITIES OF LITERATURE. 8vo, marbled boards, frontispiece of the author, decorative vellum, red and blue morocco labels, gilt, 6 vols. Ninth Edition, London, 1834.

$25.00

Doctor in Civil Law of the University of Oxford, and Fellow of the Society of Antiquaries of London, D'Israeli was a tireless bibliophile who explored many obscure and fascinating corners of literature. He gave particular attention to books of antiquity and was a very popular writer. He suffered the misfortune to become blind some nine years prior to his death. This particular work was the result of years spent among the shelves of the British Museum and secondhand book stores. Written in a delightful style, which was a contributing cause, doubtless, of the large number of reprints through which the book ran, D'Israeli records the unusual information he discovered in old books relating to forgeries and thefts, libraries, early printing and other subjects of interest to the collector. The entire set is worthy of perusal by the present day bookman. In the event, however, that the extent of the text appear too formidable, Edwin V. Mitchell of Hartford, Connecticut edited in 1932 a new one volume edition. This was published by D. Appleton Company at three dollars.

Volume 1 of this original series was first published in 1791; Volume 2 in

1793; Volume 3 in 1817; Volumes 4 and 5 in 1823 and Volume 6 in 1834. Various editions of the first series appeared from 1793 to 1841. Publication of a second series of editions began in 1823.

Du Bois, Henri P.

FOUR PRIVATE LIBRARIES OF NEW YORK, A Contribution to the History of Bibliophilism in America. First Series. Preface by Octave Uzanne. Limited to 1000 numbered copies and printed by De Vinne Press. Frontispiece and twelve other plates, demy 8vo, red silken gilt cloth, gold ornament front and back, uncut. New York, 1892.
Nos. 1 to 200 on Japanese paper
$10.00
Nos. 201 to 1000 on Holland paper
$7.50

This book has an unusual format and will delight the collector. The full page photogravure plates reproduce the bindings of famous craftsmen as well as bookplates and book illustrations.

In his introductory chapter, "The Art of the Decade," the author discusses the art of forming a library and pleads for perfection in the smallest details of collecting regardless of the subject, period or author concerned. Du Bois writes interestingly of the early bookmen, Canevari, Maioli, Grolier, Spencer, Didot and Brinley, to name a few, who "collected books like coins." He states, "They were not lovers of books; perhaps they were lovers of bibliomania."

One might gather that Du Bois was describing many present day collectors, for the faults of the fathers of book collecting have certainly been handed down. Perhaps, however, Du Bois is asking too much, for the records are full of examples of collectors who have devoted their lives to completing and perfecting their collections. Throughout the book, however, the author speaks for sincerity in collecting and for an appreciation of all that is beautiful in books.

The text of this book—and one needs a reading knowledge of French to appreciate its fullness—offers more thought-provoking material to the bibliophile than any half dozen other titles in the field of books about books, old or modern, that the writer can recall.

Duff, E. Gordon (1863-1924)

> CATALOG OF BOOKS IN THE JOHN RYLANDS LIBRARY, printed in England, Scotland and Ireland, and of books in English printed abroad to the end of the year 1640. 4to, buckram. Manchester, 1895.
> $15.00

Edward Gordon Duff was the first librarian of the John Rylands Library. This was founded by the third Mrs. Rylands a year after the death of her husband in 1888 as a memorial to him and a means of continuing her husband's work and ideals. The beautiful Gothic building in Manchester which houses the library is one of the finest pieces of architecture erected in England in the nineteenth century. It was begun in 1890 and opened in 1899. Becoming in time one of the great English libraries, it contains alone some 3000 volumes published prior to 1501.

John Rylands (1801-1888) was a successful and prosperous manufacturer of textile fabrics. Living a quiet life and deeply religious, his books reflected his individual tastes which were largely of a theological nature. Mrs. Rylands greatly augmented the original collection by purchasing in 1892 for $1,250,000 the Earl of Spencer's library, and by adding in 1892 some 6000 oriental manuscripts.

Probably few readers of this book are vitally interested as collectors in books printed in English from 1476 to 1640 with which this catalogue is mostly concerned. It is, therefore, included in this Bio-Bibliography not because of its value as a catalogue per se but mainly because it is the first published catalogue of a man who became Keeper of Printed Books at the British Museum and a most eminent bibliographical authority. In addition, the general reader and embryo collector should have some introduction to the John Rylands Library, and its first catalogue is always a good introduction to any library.

Duff's knowledge of books was broad and complete. Above all he was accurate, which is far more than can be said of most bibliographers, particularly amateur ones like the writer.

Eames, Wilberforce (1855   )

> THE FIRST YEAR OF PRINTING IN NEW YORK. May 1693 to April 1694. Illustrated with facsimiles. Royal 8vo, wrappers. New York, 1928.
> $1.00

BOOKS ABOUT BOOKS

This is an important contribution to bibliography. While the first printing for the colony of New York was in 1665, New York did not have its own printer until nearly thirty years later. Eames gives information concerning the collation and location of copies of all known publications of William Bradford.

Eames, Wilberforce (1855-   )

> BIBLIOGRAPHICAL ESSAYS—A Tribute to Wilberforce Eames, with two portraits and eight facsimiles. Royal 8vo, buckram, t.e.g. Cambridge, Mass., 1924.
> $30.00

This substantial volume of bibliographical essays edited by George Parker Winship, now assistant librarian of the Widener Library at Harvard, was prepared as a surprise and tribute to Dr. Eames without his knowledge by some thirty students and collectors. The confidential announcement of this publication reads, "as an expression of the world of students to Wilberforce Eames." Thirty-one essays of great interest are included: "The First Work with American Types" by L. C. Worth, "Wilberforce Eames, a Bio-Bibliographical Narrative" by N. H. Paltsits, "Elizabethan Americana" by G. Watson Cole, "Mills Day's Proposed Hebrew Bible" by O. Wegelin, "Sixteenth Century Mexican Imprints" by H. M. Chapin, "Some Notes on the Use of Hebrew Types In Non-Hebrew Books" by A. Marx.

Subscriptions were received in advance of publication, thirteen of which made it possible to put the manuscript through the press. Subscribers paid ten dollars each for their copies and one hundred additional copies were printed for general sale.

In addition to the wealth of material of interest to the bookman, the biographical sketch of Eames by Victor Hugo Paltsits will be an inspiration to any collector who deplores the lack of scholarship as a bar to his collecting activities. Dr. Eames himself did not enter school until nine years of age and had not more than three or four years of formal public school work. He went to work at twelve as a printer's apprentice and three years later at fifteen entered the employ of the post office. At eighteen he became a clerk in a book store and from then on his rise as an authority on bibliographical matters, despite his lack of further schooling, was rapid indeed. Dr. Eames became associated with the Lenox Library in New York in 1885 and was made librarian in 1893. When this library was merged into the New York Public Library two years later, he became Chief of the Division of American History. In 1915 he assumed the position of Bibliographer. His entire career is indicative of what can be accomplished in a highly technical field of scholarship provided one has earnestness of purpose and strength of will diligently to apply oneself. He was awarded the gold medal of the Bibliographical Society of London in 1929.

As a text book on practical bibliography and as a source of information on the interests of its collective authors who are in themselves specialists in bibliography, this volume cannot be matched. Because of this as well as in honor of Dr. Eames, it should find a place in the hands and on the shelves of all sincere collectors.

Eckel, John C. (1858-   )

PRIME PICKWICKS IN PARTS. Census with Complete Collation, Comparison and Comment. With a Foreword by A. Edward Newton. Illustrated, 8vo., cloth, limited to 440 copies signed by Mr. Eckel and Mr. Newton. New York, 1928.

$30.00

It was not the intention of the writer to include in this volume any bibliographies of individual authors. As, however, the works of Charles Dickens bid fair to remain collectors' items for some time to come, this bibliography warrants due mention. Tribute is paid its author who is an unquestioned Dickens' authority and a bookseller of note. Furthermore, the preface alone by A. Edward Newton, best known of American collectors, merits the attention of the reader.

Edwards, Edward (1812-1887)

MEMOIRS OF LIBRARIES, including a handbook of Library Economy, frontispiece, 6 folding plates, 18 full page plates, 4 colored and 2 other plates of book-bindings, numerous text illustrations 2 vols., royal 8vo, cloth. London, 1859

$12.50

Aside from its general interest to any lover of books, this item is described here, not because of its particular value to the book collector of today, but in order to add a bit to the recollection and memory of the man who made it possible for the English people to enjoy free public libraries. While England has never had a Carnegie, whose liberality was able to extend the benefits of free libraries far beyond Edwards' expectations, she did have in Edwards a man who in continual self-effacement worked unceasingly, and successfully, to provide libraries for the lasting benefit of his countrymen.

Edwards' life as a personal career was a most distressing failure and he died horribly in the extreme poverty in which most of his life had been lived. His work, however, is indicative of his earnestness of purpose and is beautiful in its spiritual qualities. Seeing no hope ahead, Edwards underlined in his Bible, which he continually studied, the words, "They shall hunger no more, neither thirst no more," and then wrote the date, "July 20, 1885, 9:30, A.M."

The story of Edwards' death would arouse the sympathy of any man but is of particular distress to those, who, because of their own literary interests, can appreciate the position and state of mind in which he found himself. Near the close of his life, Edwards retired, on a government pension of eighty pounds a year, to a cottage at Niton on the Isle of Wight. He had completed his work and the world was done with him. His fellow villagers knew him only as a solitary old man of dignified manner and good habits. In debt for printing and postage, his necessities accumulated. It became impossible for him to pay his house rent and he was reduced to actual want. For some months he was housed with the Baptist minister of the village, a Mr. Harrison. One morning in November a small bill was presented which he could not pay. Telling his kind host that he was going on a visit to a nearby town, he left by coach and was found some days afterward in a roofless ruin on St. Catherine's Down where he had spent three bitter cold nights without food or shelter. It was only the warmth of the sheep which preserved his life. He never recovered from the exposure and died early in the following year.

Egan, Maurice F. (1852-1894)

CONFESSIONS OF A BOOK LOVER. 8vo, blue cloth, paper label. New York, 1922.

$2.50

Mr. Egan covers within this book a wide range of reading. He has a sense of humor and his comments are interesting. His experiences with the literature of the world are indicative of the results of the sound foundation he laid in his early reading which began with his boyhood. This is an excellent book with

THE BIO-BIBLIOGRAPHY

which to add to one's general knowledge of what should be read to acquire any understanding at all of much of the best that has been produced in literature.

Starting with the Bible, which, incidentally, in its various printings, has long been a collector's item that has undoubtedly been studied more carefully by bookmen than by those who wear the cloth, Egan introduces his readers to the great essayists, poets, novelists, and biographers. Too much homage cannot be paid these men who with their minds and pens have created the books that have become with the years so much a part and parcel of our lives.

Evans, Charles (1850-1935)

AMERICAN BIBLIOGRAPHY, A Chronological Dictionary of all Books, Pamphlets and Periodical Publications Printed in the United States of America from the Genesis in 1639 down to and including the Year 1820. Vols. 1-12, Chicago, 1903-1934.

$200.00

Evans' AMERICAN BIBLIOGRAPHY has often been called the "Old Bookseller's Bible" for it is usually the first reference manual a dealer will consult when he has reason to suspect that he has acquired a rare and valuable American book. After sixteen years of preparatory work, the first volume appeared in 1903. The arrangement, as is necessary in a work of this kind, is chronological, although the separate years are arranged alphabetically. Cross indices in each volume will supply the reader with references to authors, places and subjects. Twelve quarto volumes bringing the record down to 1799 have been issued so far.

Charles Evans was born in Boston, November 11, 1850 and received his education in the public schools of that city. He began his bibliographical work as an assistant in the Boston Athenaeum Library, a post he held from 1886 to 1892. A founder of the American Library Association, he was a member both active and honorary of many other libraries and library organizations.

In the early months of 1902, Evans issued a circular outlining his plans for the publication of this work. At the time, he was secretary and librarian of the Chicago Historical Society and had long given considerable thought to an elaborate and comprehensive American bibliography. As his circular stated, this was to be "a chronological dictionary of all books, pamphlets and periodical publications printed in the United States of America, from the genesis of printing in 1639 down to and including the year 1820, with bibliographical and biographical notes." Evans thought that the entire work would comprise six volumes and it was his intention to have one appear each year. It is interesting to note that the work, instead of covering six years, has kept Evans almost continually occupied since 1902.

The compilation and publication was undertaken as a private enterprise to be sold by subscription only at a price of $15 per volume. Each volume was to be signed and numbered. Evans estimated that 70,000 titles would be included. Three hundred copies of Volumes I to VIII, covering the years 1639-1792, were privately printed by the author from 1903 to 1914. These copies were sold mostly to libraries. During the war period, publication was suspended, but in 1924, through the cooperation of the American Library Association, Volume IX was issued and since then three more have appeared, making a total of twelve to date.

Fabes, Gilbert (1894-   )

MODERN FIRST EDITIONS, POINTS AND VALUES, First Series. Medium 8vo, buckram, gilt, one of 750 copies. London, 1929.

$7.50

First issued in 1929 this work had up to 1932 been continued through three volumes to complete the trilogy of bibliographical revelations as conceived by Mr. Fabes. This book and the other two volumes in the series comprise an essential work for those interested in modern first editions. There is included an interesting Introduction. One hundred titles are dealt with in this initial volume.

Ferguson, John (1837-1916)

SOME ASPECTS OF BIBLIOGRAPHY. Square 8vo, blue cloth, paper label, large paper, limited to 26 copies. Edinburgh, 1900.

$25.00

In addition to this beautiful limited edition, which has the widest letter press margins the writer has ever seen, a trade edition of 300 copies was also printed. A copy of this later edition is valued at $7.50.

This treatise on bibliography originated as a farewell address on the occasion of Ferguson's vacating the Presidency of the Edinburgh Bibliographical Society on November 2, 1898. It was not published, however, until two years later in October 1900. Sir William Osler, who was at his death President of the London Bibliographical Society, considered this the best introductory manual he knew on the subject.

Field, Eugene (1850-1895)

> LOVE AFFAIRS OF A BIBLIOMANIAC, with a preface by Roswell M. Field. 12mo, boards, vellum back, large paper, one of 100 copies. New York, 1896.
> $12.00

This book, which has been described as the best American essay on book collecting, is an example of true bibliophilism. It is not distorted by expressions of financial frenzy. It is semi-humorous but contains an interesting account of many of the books that Field collected. It was the last book he wrote, being published posthumously.

Eugene Field was best known for his column, "Sharps and Flats," that appeared for the twelve years prior to his death in the *Chicago Daily News*. For this column which attracted readers the country over, Field wrote approximately twenty-three hundred words a day. This is twice the output of most present day columnists. Largely the originator of this type of newspaper writing, he was paid upon the same relative basis that most pioneers in any field of endeavor are paid. His maximum salary was $52.50 a week.

Born in St. Louis, Field attended Williams and Knox Colleges as well as the University of Missouri but never for a period of longer than six months. He failed consequently to get a degree but this omission did nothing to detract from his subsequent literary career.

Fitzgerald, Percy (1834-   )

> THE BOOK FANCIER or The Romance of Book-Collecting. 12mo, green cloth, t.e.g. First edition, London, 1886.
> $3.00

This little volume with its chapters on Book-Collectors and Dealers, Incunabulas, Caxtons, Bindings, Illustrated Books, etc., is typical of the hodge-podge fashion in which many volumes on book collecting have been written. The book is of interest because it is indicative of the subjects which held the attention of the amateur collector at the time of its publication. No mention is made of the authors of Fitzgerald's day.

That Oscar Wilde, a contemporary of Fitzgerald, was also an earnest bookman is indicated by his following harsh criticism of this book. "He, Fitzgerald, talks of Grolier as a bookbinder; he is eloquent over a Shakespearean quarto TAMING OF THE SHREW, though there is no such book in existence; he tells that the first edition of PARADISE LOST is procurable in small folio, a statement that will amaze Mr. Quaritch; and informs us that Valdefar's edition of BOCCACCIO, a book published in 1471, was very scarce in the beginning of the 15th century, a time when printing was not yet invented, etc." Nevertheless, in spite of Wilde's severe review, the book is a collector's item.

Fletcher, W. Y. (1830-1913)

> ENGLISH BOOK COLLECTORS, illustrated with fine portraits, book stamps and engravings. Square 8vo, vellum, t.e.g., one of 50 copies on Japanese paper. London, 1902.
> $12.50

An account of famous English book collectors, including John Bagford, Beckford, Dr. Dee, Kearne, Heber, Locker-Lamson, Robert Harley, Horace Walpole, Royal Collectors and others. In this volume of some 400 pages, collectors of manuscripts or bookmen like Bodely, who collected solely with the thought of forming a public library, have been eliminated. As a result, only those collectors who bought books simply for their personal enjoyment and the satisfaction of their immediate requirements are considered.

Unlike the representatives of some other forms of activity, book collectors are generally of engaging personality and strong individualists. This statement is witnessed by a consideration of the collectors of the present day whose names are often in the public prints and is especially true of the bibliophiles Fletcher describes, beginning with Bishop Fisher in the sixteenth century and ending with William Morris in the nineteenth.

Thirty years ago, any paper pertaining to the general subject of book collecting might well and correctly state that this particular form of madness among men took root at the end of the seventeenth century and flowered in its prime during the eighteenth century. Dibdin, as a matter of fact, makes the statement that book collecting reached its peak in 1813. We may charitably refrain, out of respect for the memory of one of the greatest writers on bookish subjects, from any comment on the increasing activity in the sale of rare books which has taken place since Dibdin's time and which he entirely failed to forecast. However, Dibdin cannot be too easily censored, for certainly it was during the eighteenth century that men became more prominently identified with the collecting of books than at any previous time.

It is difficult to give an adequate account of Fletcher's ENGLISH BOOK COLLECTORS because of the book's unusual combination of the features of a dictionary and catalogue as well as a biography. The student and collector, however, will find that it contains many interesting accounts of the historical background of collecting and the parts that certain individuals played in it during their time. The lives and characteristics of the great collectors provide a fine series of biographical sketches, while the descriptions of their libraries, methods of collecting and alphabetical lists of sales are indicative of the fact that bookmen then as now enjoyed their delightful hobby as only a book hunter can.

Fleuron, The

> THE FLEURON, A Journal of Typography, edited by Oliver Simon. Numerous illustrations, 4to, cloth back, paper boards. No. 1, London, 1923. Out of print and scarce. $22.50

As a source of information on modern typography for the seven year period 1923-1930, the articles in the yearly volumes of THE FLEURON are indispensable. They originated as a result of the efforts on the part of a group of English typographers and artists to apply the principles of design and common sense to printing of today. They should hold an undisputed place in the collector's reference library. The historical side of printing has by no means been neglected by the editors, and an excellent background of the progress of fine printing can be secured from a perusal of these volumes.

Mr. Oliver Simon whose editorial activities first made these articles available to students, collectors and lovers of printing, deserves, as does Stanley Morrison, who in later years carried on the work, considerable credit for the selection of material as well as for the choice of authors who are represented.

Outstanding bookmen, designers, collectors and writers of books about books are included among the authors of THE FLEURON. Among them are the names of

BOOKS ABOUT BOOKS

T. M. Cleland, Paul Beaujon, D. B. Updike, Karl Klingspor, Eric Gill, Bruce Rogers, Frederic Warde, Holbrook Jackson, Stanley Morrison, Francis Meynell and others who are distinguished for their contributions to the art of the printed word.

There has been no American publication comparable to THE FLEURON. THE COLOPHON comes nearest to approaching it and in many respects the First Series does surpass even the de luxe editions of THE FLEURON in the beauty of its make-up and typography. THE COLOPHON, however, is essentially a medium devoted to the interests of the book collector rather than to those of the cultivated amateur and the professional typographer.

A great deal has been done by DeVinne, McMurtrie, Updike, and Orcutt to arouse a popular interest in fine printing in our own country. They sowed good seed which it is hoped the next generation of bookmen may earnestly cultivate to the end that enough devotees of printing as an art as well as a business will exist to make possible the publication and support of a yearly journal similar in character to THE FLEURON at its best.

Foley, Patrick K.

AMERICAN AUTHORS 1795-1895, A Bibliography of First and Notable Editions Chronologically Arranged with Notes. Introduction by Walter Leon Sawyer of Boston. Printed for subscribers, Boston, 1897.
$25.00

The same, large paper
$35.00

This bibliography of Foley's has long been the cornerstone of many a library devoted to Americana. Five hundred copies of the work were issued and they were quickly sold. As a reference book for collectors and dealers it was recognized as being without equal. In fact the book was unique, for it was the only one of its kind in print at the time of publication, and did much to stimulate an interest in the early printing and first editions of this country. R. W. G. Vail, Librarian of the American Antiquarian Society, says it is "still the best book [in its reference field] in spite of its age."

Undoubtedly it was the means of attracting many new collectors to American authors. Mr. Foley rendered yeoman service to the cause of American bibliography if only from the standpoint of the notable unknown works he uncovered in the course of research incidental to the preparation of his book.

Although badly needed, no revised edition of Foley's work has appeared. It is understood, however, that at least one bibliographer, Donald Coney, of the School of Library Science at the University of North Carolina, is working at the task.

Collectors and dealers probably owe more to Foley than to any other man, for he provided them with an authoritative bibliographical tool. He was called "Columbus of First Editions," for recording more valuable unknown works of American authors than anyone before him. For a time, "Not in Foley" became a by-word on the lips of dealers and in their own and auction catalogues. Naturally, in later years Mr. Foley and others found many new items by American authors, so the phrase was discarded. Foley not only stimulated a new interest among collectors but also was the means of starting many a collector in the realm of Americana.

Garnett Richard (1866-1906)

LIBRARY SERIES, Edited by Sir Richard Garnett. 4 vols., 8vo., green cloth. London, 1899.

$15.00

The volumes included in the above set are LIBRARY ADMINISTRATION by John Macfarlane, late staff member of the British Museum, PRICES OF BOOKS by Henry B. Wheatley, THE FREE LIBRARY by John J. Ogle, and the editor's ESSAYS IN LIBRARIANSHIP AND BIBLIOGRAPHY.

Richard Garnett was one time Keeper of Printed Books of the British Museum. During his stewardship, his encouragement and interest brought about a great activity that gave to other bibliographical writers an impetus to their work that has proved an inspiration ever since to the members of their craft.

Gentleman's Magazine

THE GENTLEMAN'S MAGAZINE LIBRARY, being a classified collection of the chief contents of the Gentleman's Magazine from 1731 to 1868, edited by George Lawrence Gomme, together with Bibliographical Notes edited by A. C. Buckley. 8vo, uncut. London, 1888.

$5.00

BOOKS ABOUT BOOKS

The purpose of the editor of this volume was to collect from the pages of THE GENTLEMAN'S MAGAZINE articles and facts relative to the history of bookmaking, bookselling, libraries, and other bibliographical information of interest and value to the collector. The volume is filled with material of an instructive nature, although, naturally, much of it is of no current value to the present day bookman.

Within its covers will be found considerable data previously scattered and hidden among the many volumes of its original publication.

Graham, Bessie (1883-   )

THE BOOKMAN'S MANUAL, A Guide to Literature. 8vo, blue cloth. Third edition, revised and enlarged, New York, 1928.

$4.00

Miss Graham has provided in this volume of thirty-two chapters a vast amount of information regarding the source books or books of reference in various fields of literature. The MANUAL which is an expansion of the chapter, "Bibliography in Literature," in Adolph Growoll's book, THE PROFESSION OF BOOKSELLING, was first published in 1921. A second edition appeared in 1924. The book is most useful to the dealer who must have somewhat more than a superficial knowledge of the various classes of books he is handling. It is likewise of great value to the collector and general reader who needs a working background of the landmarks of literature, of what they consist, their purpose and where to find them.

Certain branches such as children's books, economics, sociology and travel, to name a few, have been omitted as even minor bibliographies of these subjects would constitute whole books in themselves. Miss Graham has rightly confined her discussion to the fields of pure literature, biography, drama, the classics, poetry, history, art, music, etc., which have a historical background.

Greaves, Haslehurst

THE PERSONAL LIBRARY, How To Make and How to Use It. 12mo, cloth. London, 1928.

$1.50

The author of this little treatise succeeds in the course of some ninety-four pages in imparting to his readers his own sense of delight in the collecting and

THE BIO-BIBLIOGRAPHY

preserving of books. Not everyone will agree with his recommendations and comments, but this may likewise be said of the conclusions of every writer on bookish subjects. The brief chapter on auction sales and book collecting will probably be found the most interesting and helpful to the average student who still feels the need of elementary instruction in the art of collecting.

It is undoubtedly a waste of time for the majority of readers to be told again by Mr. Greaves that a book is not necessarily valuable because it is old, and yet this statement is quite worth repeating, for few people seem to appreciate this first principle regardless of how often and by how many different writers it is stated. Unfortunately, at least from the writer's point of view, it seems that most of Mr. Greaves' counsel is given with the thought in mind of the collector who is to buy books as a speculation rather than through the eyes of the man who is making a collection for its own sake and his own pleasure.

A careful collection of books, almost regardless of the authors or subjects represented, is by no means to be ignored as a feature in the spending of one's income. Many times it has been shown that a collector's books were the only tangible asset of his estate. After all, books cannot dissipate as can cash or securities. However, if one is to speculate, let him buy common stocks in which the rate of turnover, even in the dullest times, is somewhat more rapid than is the market for rare books.

One of the greatest difficulties encountered as a collection grows is the increasing inability to keep it properly arranged and catalogued in order that each book or pamphlet may be instantly at hand when required. Mr. Greaves' instructions on the care and cataloguing of a library will be helpful to the collector who is so disposed to arrange his books. One is to be cautioned, however, about having too elaborate a system, or one which, because of the labor involved in keeping it up to date, would in any way detract from the pleasure of the books themselves. After all, a private collection, no matter how large, is a far more intimate matter than the coldly catalogued books in our public institutions.

Not the least interesting section of Mr. Greaves' book is the introduction by Mr. Gilbert H. Fabes, himself a writer of books about books. In discussing the book which we have for the moment under consideration, he says, "The dominant idea of this useful book is the making and using of a personal library, and the literature of books about books is enriched by its arrival. The side paths and the pitfalls, the fascinations and the heartburnings are all other chapters of which more and more remain to be written."

BOOKS ABOUT BOOKS

Grolier, Jean (1479-1565)

> RESEARCHES CONCERNING JEAN GROLIER, His Life and His Library, with a partial catalogue of his books by J. V. Le Roux De Lincy, edited by Baron R. Portalis of the Société des Bibliophiles Français. Originally printed by Jouaust, Paris, 1866. Translated and revised by Carolyn Shipman, member, Bibliographical Society of London. Magnificently illustrated in color. Thick imperial 8vo, half blue morocco, uncut. Limited to 300 copies on unbleached, handmade paper. The Grolier Club, New York, 1907.
>
> $35.00

It is fitting that the Grolier Club, bearing the name of the founder of the French school of ornamental binding, should cause to be reprinted this memoir of his life and work. One purpose of Le Roux De Lincy was to compile a complete catalogue of Grolier's extant works. He spent fifteen years on the task, his finished work being published, as noted above, in 1866. This reprint was issued in 1907 to celebrate the twentieth anniversary of the Grolier Club.

Grolier, who remained throughout his life a patron of the book trade in all its phases, was born at Lyons in 1479. He became Treasurer-General of France in 1547 and was a man of considerable wealth. He was well able to indulge his fancy in the superb bindings easily recognizable today. They always bore, so far as is known, the inscription, IO GROLERII ET AMICORUM. Grolier died in 1565 and is buried before the main altar of the Church of the Abbey S. Germain des Prés in Paris, a church to which he was always devoted.

The Grolier Club in New York City which has sponsored so many fine publications houses a splendid library of 20,000 volumes, the nucleus of which is one of the greatest collections pertaining to bibliography and books about books. The club has done much to encourage a lively interest in books of all kinds and in particular has made possible important researches in the field of bibliography. It was founded at the home of Robert Hoe on January 23, 1884 with an initial membership of nine. The library is open not only to members but to all earnest students of book history and production. The club's own series of publications constitute a valuable addition to the literature of books about books. Exhibits of rare books of typographical interest are held periodically. The public is admitted without charge.

Hain, Ludwig (1781-1836)

> REPERTORIUM BIBLIOGRAPHICUM, in quo Libri Omnes ab Arte Typographica inventa usque ad annum M D, Typis Erpressi ordine alphabetico vel simpliciter enumerantur. 4 vols., half morocco. Stuttgart, 1826-1838.
>
> $70.00

This is the most important of the bibliographies of incunabula, containing 16,299 entries. It is a true source book and indispensable to any collector or collection of fifteenth century books. All dealers' library catalogues as well as bibliographies dealing in incunabula constantly refer to Hain. Dr. Konrad Burger added in 1891 an Index of Printers to Hain's work. During the period 1898-1902, Dr. W. Copinger computed and published a supplement and upwards of 7000 additional descriptions. In 1908 another supplement was added by Dr. Burger and in 1905-1911 various appendices and an index were provided by Dr. Dietrich Reichling.

Few if any of the readers of this book will be vitally interested in, or collectors of, incunabula. To concentrate upon the purchase of books printed before the year 1500 would require a sizeable purse and except as curiosities these books are best left to the librarians and other experts. To obtain an accurate working knowledge of the subject of fifteenth century books is the task of a lifetime. There is a fascination about them, however, for most book collectors, and one must have a certain familiarity with them. After all, they constitute the earliest form of the printed book and their conception was the foundation upon which book collecting was established.

Any bibliography of books about books must include Hain who provided for collectors the first scientific bibliography of incunabula.

Hazlitt, William Carew (1834-1913)

> THE CONFESSIONS OF A COLLECTOR. 8vo, buckram. London, 1897.
>
> $3.50

Hazlitt's experiences as a collector extended over a period of many years. His book which is autobiographical in form contains many interesting reminiscences of collectors and dealers of his day. Hazlitt attributes his interest in books entirely to heredity and holds his father responsible for making him, instead of a distinguished civil servant or a successful professional man, a bibliographer, collector and antiquary.

For some ten years or more, Hazlitt was a buyer of books for Henry Huth and to a large extent was instrumental in enlarging and cataloguing Huth's great collection. In the latter task, he was associated with Mr. F. S. Ellis, the London bookseller. Unfortunately, differences of opinion arose between Mr. Huth and Hazlitt, and for several years prior to Mr. Huth's death in 1878 they were not on the intimate standing of former years.

As a glance at the index will indicate, the reader will find in this volume anecdotes of Hazlitt's contemporaries, among whom were Locker-Lamson, Christie-Miller, Henry Pyne and Elliot Stock. Among the principal booksellers of the day with whom Hazlitt traded, were Joseph Lilly, Bernard Quaritch, F. S. Ellis, B. M. Pickering, John Pearson and Willis and Sotheran.

Hart, Horace

BIBLIOTHECA TYPOGRAPHICA, A List of Books about Books, with an Introduction by George Parker Winship. 8vo, cloth, half morocco, t.e.g., boxed. Limited to 250 copies signed by the author. Rochester, 1933.
$5.00

The author of this book at the time of its compilation was a Harvard undergraduate. His publishers stated in their announcement circular that the work would be a "concise, comprehensive and completely modern list of books about books." Of the items described under bibliography and book collecting with which readers are principally concerned, seventy-seven separate books are listed. This number by no means represents a complete list, but within the limited field of modern books on these subjects, the author has done an honest piece of work.

Mention must be made of the general attractiveness of the volume, for in its binding and typography it is a splendid example of present day printing and of binding of a commercial nature made to sell at a reasonable figure.

For those desiring a working bibliography embracing the history of writing and printing from the development of the alphabet through the science of bibliography and the art of book collecting, this work of Mr. Hart's will serve as an admirable guide. A trade edition was issued at two dollars and a half.

Hoe, Robert (1839-1909)

> THE LIBRARY OF ROBERT HOE, The complete priced SALE CATALOGUE, 8 parts in paper covers. The Anderson Auction Company, New York, 1911-12.
> $45.00

The Hoe Library was unquestionably one of the finest in the world. This CATALOGUE with the sale prices of nearly 15,000 items ranging from the fifteenth to the twentieth century is an invaluable bibliography for the collector. The library was rich in Manuscripts, Incunabula, Bindings, English Literature, French Books, Americana and Autographs.

An outstanding feature of the Hoe Sale was the part played by Henry E. Huntington, founder of the great library in San Marino, California which bears his name, as the largest individual purchaser. Aided by the late George D. Smith, who as a bookseller was at the height of his fame, Mr. Huntington took advantage of the opportunity to secure for his own library, regardless of price, many of the choicest books.

In his time and for over a span of fifty years, Robert Hoe was the greatest collector the country produced. He was a man of wealth but had as well the knowledge and taste that enabled him to amass his library. Fortunately, Hoe threw no boundaries around his collecting activities. No definite plan limited his purchases except his unrelenting standard of quality. The result was that few monuments of literature regardless of author or subject were lacking in his collection. Mr. Beverly Chew, himself a noted collector, wrote a fine appreciation of Hoe which will be found as a Foreword in Part 1 of the CATALOGUE.

Ireland, Alexander (1810-1894)

> THE BOOK-LOVER'S ENCHIRIDON, A Treasury of Thoughts on the Solace and Companionship of Books. 4to, green cloth, t.e.g., uncut, large paper copy. Fifth edition, London, 1888.
> $7.50

This book was first printed in 1882 but the fifth edition described above is considered the best. It has proved a most popular book among collectors and general readers and is frequently quoted in the writings of current authors of books about books.

BOOKS ABOUT BOOKS

Two pocket sized editions were printed within a few months of each other in the first year of publication. These measured 4¼ by 3 inches. A third edition of 4000 copies was issued in 1883. This edition was very favorably received and in 1884 a fourth edition, considerably revised and enlarged, of 5000 copies was printed only to be followed four years later by the edition described above.

THE BOOK-LOVERS ENCHIRIDON is a fine example of an earnest and carefully prepared book for the collector and bookman. One can sense the pleasure of the author in its compilation. He succeeded admirably in providing a work of inspiration to meet the moods and needs of thoughtful minds, which, as Ireland says in his preface to the fifth edition, "seek in books, not amusement or mere passive enjoyment but the inspiration and quickening influence of high aims and noble purposes."

In compiling this book, the author did a really remarkable piece of work in that he quotes in chronological order from Solomon, born in 1033 B.C., to Richard Le Gallienne, born in 1866 A.D., the references made to the love and value of books by the foremost and wisest minds. For example, the following from Richard Baxter (1615-1691) will evoke a warm response in present day readers just as it undoubtedly did some three centuries ago. It is interesting to note that what Baxter said appeared in a religious publication known as the CHRISTIAN DIRECTORY:

"But books have the advantage in many other respects: You may read an able preacher, when you have but a mean one to hear. Every congregation cannot hear the most judicious or powerful preachers; but every single person may read the books of the most powerful and judicious. Preachers may be silenced or banished when books may be at hand; books may be kept at a smaller charge than preachers; we may choose books which treat of that very subject which we desire to hear of; but we cannot choose what subject the preacher shall treat of. Books we may have at hand every day and every hour; when we can have sermons but seldom, and at set times. If sermons be forgotten, they are gone. But a book we may read over and over until we remember it; and, if we forget it, may again peruse it at our pleasure or at our leisure, so that good books are a very great mercy to the world."

Jackson, Holbrook (1874-   )

THE ANATOMY OF BIBLIOMANIA. 2 vols., Demy 8vo, full morocco, gilt. One of 48 copies on hand made paper signed by the author. London, 1931. $65.00

THE BIO-BIBLIOGRAPHY

> Another copy. 2 vols., 8vo., cloth, 1000 copies printed. New York, 1931.
>
> $22.50
>
> Another edition. 1 vol., 8vo., buckram. New York and London.
>
> $5.00

A. Edward Newton has been quoted so often in reference to this book that it will do no harm to draw on him once more. He says in the *Atlantic Monthly*, "Of all the books in praise of books ever written, this is the most exhaustive and the best. One wonders if Jackson be a man or a whole regiment of men. It would seem that no man's reading could have been so extensive. One does not get such a book out of a library; one must own it, if one has to steal it."

THE ANATOMY OF BIBLIOMANIA is probably the most complete book on the subject of book madness ever written although its text, with constant references and footnotes, will be found a bit difficult to read. It is not an entertaining book but rather an instructive one that requires extremely careful concentration.

It will, undoubtedly, become a classic and should be in the hands of every collector. The writer is inclined to wish, however, that Jackson had not borrowed the style of writing affected by Robert Burton in his Anatomy of Melancholy.

Johnson, A. F.

> ONE HUNDRED TITLE PAGES 1500-1800, Selected and Arranged with Introduction and Notes. Frontispiece and numerous illustrations, 4to, boards, cloth back. London, 1928.
>
> $7.50

Mr. Johnson wrote this while Assistant Keeper of printed books in the British Museum. From the resources available to him, he has pictured, through a splendid collection of examples, the evolution of the title page. His book reveals how early typographers met the practical problems of their day.

Johnson, Merle de Vore (1874-   )

> AMERICAN FIRST EDITIONS, A Bibliographical Check List of the Works of 105 American Authors. One of 1000 copies printed by D. B. Updike at the Merrymount Press

BOOKS ABOUT BOOKS

for R. R. Bowker Company, Royal 8vo, New York, 1928. First edition, out of print.
$15.00

Second edition, revised and enlaregd, 1932.
$5.00

Third edition, revised and enlarged by Jacob Blanch, 8vo, buckram. New York, 1936.
$10.00

The writer has said that P. K. Foley's AMERICAN AUTHORS, published in 1897, probably did more to stimulate book collecting than any previously published bibliographical guide. What a boon that book was to dealers upon its publication! Now comes Mr. Johnson with the apparent thought in mind of carrying on where Foley left off. Whether AMERICAN FIRST EDITIONS will become within its range a standard reference source comparable with Foley's work, only time can tell. The book represents, however, a sincere attempt to be of substantial help to the collector. From a perusal of its pages, one will become acquainted with a number of authors who have exerted a considerable influence on the literature of our country. Both Mr. Foley's work and Mr. Johnson's have served to call the attention of collector and of dealer alike to authors who are little known and whose books may well be worth the attention of the discriminating buyer.

In a work embracing such a large field and so many individual authors, it was not feasible to go into detail with respect to many bibliographical points, and in the main the book serves primarily as a check list. Sufficient information is given in every instance, however, to enable the dealer or collector to identify a first edition of any of the authors included. The book is compact and well arranged with authors listed alphabetically.

Mr. Johnson has done an excellent piece of work and the book will prove a useful addition to the working library of the experienced collector as well as a good introduction to the American field for the young enthusiast.

Johnson, S.

THE R. B. ADAM LIBRARY RELATING TO DR. SAMUEL JOHNSON AND HIS ERA. Numerous plates, illustrations of portraits and views, facsimiles of manuscripts and printed books. 3 vols., 4to, cloth. Buffalo, 1929.
$50.00

THE BIO-BIBLIOGRAPHY

For a catalogue of a collection devoted to a single author, this work ranks as number one. This great Adam Library was begun by Mr. Robert B. Adam, a native of Scotland who settled in Buffalo, New York in 1867. He lived to the age of seventy-three, dying in 1904. His Johnson collection was continued by the publisher of the CATALOGUE, Mr. R. B. Adam II, who was the nephew and adopted son of the founder.

Mr. A. Edward Newton, himself one of the most noted of present day collectors whose activities are related at varying places throughout this Bio-Bibliography, contributes a charming preface to the work. There is also an introductory essay in the first volume by Dr. Charles G. Osgood of Princeton University.

Reviewing the CATALOGUE at the time of its publication, George H. Sargent called special attention to the delightful introduction by Dr. Osgood, in the course of which he stated that no one except Johnson himself would be qualified to speak adequately of the Adam collection. The writer confesses to a similar feeling of inadequacy with respect to this brief sketch.

The entire work is beautifully illustrated with numerous plates, portraits of Dr. Johnson, views of Litchfield and of Johnson's London. Containing as it does so many of Johnson's letters and manuscripts as well as letters of Boswell, the volumes constitute, to a certain extent, a biography of the great doctor. The first volume is devoted to material of this nature. The second volume is a bibliography of Johnson, illustrated with many facsimiles of manuscripts, printed sheets and title pages. The third volume is devoted largely to a catalogue and texts of letters of Johnson's friends and contemporaries such as Garrick, Goldsmith, Gay, Sheridan, Macaulay, Gainsborough, Rubens and Descartes.

Jordan-Smith, Paul (1885-   )

FOR THE LOVE OF BOOKS, The Adventures of an Impecunious Collector. 8vo, black and tan boards, gilt, t.e.g. Illustrated. New York, 1934.

$2.50

For the collector who is interested in the books of contemporary American and English authors, Mr. Jordan-Smith has produced an interesting volume of literary criticism. As the literary editor and critic of the *Los Angeles Times*, he had plenty of material to draw upon, and it will be found particularly helpful to students who are searching for a source of information concerning many of the modern authors to whom they have been drawn.

Kern, Jerome (1856-)

> CATALOGUE OF THE SALE OF THE LIBRARY OF JEROME KERN sold at auction by the Anderson Galleries January 7-10 and January 21-24, 1929, with prices marked. 2 vols., 4to, paper wrappers. New York, 1929.
>
> $10.00

This catalogue of the great Kern Sale, at which over $1,700,000 was realized, is included in order that readers not already familiar with the fact of the sale may know of a source from which they may secure a picture of the extent reached by the demand for first editions and rare books at the peak of the most recent collecting craze.

Jerome Kern, a brilliant musical composer and author of such smash song hits as are included in the musical scores of *Show Boat* and *Roberta*, also found time to amass, within a decade, a most extraordinary collection of English and American first editions. In the selection of the individual items that comprised his library, he showed the same understanding of popular appreciation as is evident in his musical compositions, for, when placed upon the market, collectors and dealers forced prices to an unprecedented extent in their eagerness to own his books.

It must be remembered that at the time of the Kern Sale, the United States was approaching the peak of the greatest boom in business, stock market and commodity prices the country had ever known. Kern anticipated the crash that came in October of 1929 and undoubtedly, by offering his library in January, sold out at exactly the right time.

Few people, either before or since that date, could afford to pay the prices reached. The spread between purchase and sale price was, in most instances, something at which to marvel. A TOM JONES, for example, purchased for $3,000 sold at $27,500. Shelley's QUEEN MAB, with his own manuscript, notes and revisions, jumped from $12,000 to $68,000.

The Kern Sale marked the beginning of a period of much lower prices for books that are known as rare. The trend now, however, seems to have turned again in an upward direction and there is no question but what ultimately the prices established at the Kern Sale will, in turn, be surpassed.

Keynes, Geoffrey Langdon (1887-   )

> WILLIAM PICKERING, PUBLISHER, A Memoir and a Handlist of his Editions. Facsimiles of thirty-seven title-pages, eight in color. 4to, cloth, wrappers, limited to 350 copies. Printed by the Chiswick Press; published by The Fleuron, London and by the Medici Society, London, 1924. $10.00

That William Pickering (1796-1854) was famous as a designer and producer of books has long been known to most collectors, but the scope of his influence on the history of the book trade in England has not been fully appreciated. Mr. Keynes' monograph gives considerable information on this point. He has written an excellent short biography of Pickering, giving an account of his activities as a publisher and bookseller. A hand-list of the principle publications from Pickering's press is also included and thirty of his most effective title pages are reproduced in order to show his skill as a book designer.

During the first half of the nineteenth century, William Pickering probably did more than any other single man to raise the standard of book production. The trade even to this day owes a great deal to his enterprise. He showed an impeccable taste not only in the publishing of books but as a collector in the acquiring of his private library, the sale of which after his death occupied three days. The illegitimate son of "a book-loving earl and his mother a lady of title," Pickering's interest in books was inherited. He was given the name of the tailor in whose family he was reared. As a boy of fourteen, he was apprenticed to a bookseller and at twenty-four, with a capital of £1000 provided by his father, he entered upon his own business career as an antiquarian bookseller. In spite of his increasing labors as a publisher, he never gave up his book shop in which, in the course of years, he accumulated a large and varied stock indicative of a great range of scholarship.

Pickering's reprints, especially his editions of the classics, were notable. His first volume, Richard Baxter's POETICAL FRAGMENTS, appearing in 1821 was bound in cloth with a paper label. This is the first ascertainable instance of the use of cloth for a binding. He adopted as his device or colophon the dolphin and anchor of Aldus (1450-1515), the founder of that great and historic Italian printing house. It is the opinion of the writer that in his handling of the traditions of his predecessors, Pickering was justified in bringing to life again this most noted of all printer's emblems.

BOOKS ABOUT BOOKS

Koch, Theodore Wesley (1871-)

> THE MIRROR OF THE PARISIAN BIBLIOPHILE, A Satirical Tale by Alfred Bonnardot. 8vo., blue cloth, gold title, decorative boards. Chicago, 1931.
> $12.50

Due credit is here given a translator rather than the author. The French original, of which only 160 copies were printed in 1848, is little known. Dr. Koch, the eminent head of the library at Northwestern University, has produced a delightful translation of this gay tale of rivalry between two Parisian collectors. The story is replete with the jargon of the booksellers and the psychology of the collector. The moral Bonnardot drew from his tale seems to be that one devoted to the worship of books must remain a bachelor or, as Koch says, "risk an almost inevitable misfortune, for a woman's heart cannot tolerate the rivalry of a favorite library." Any ardent present-day collector can testify to the truthfulness of this statement.

This book is the fifth of Dr. Koch's translations of tales for bibliophiles, another in the series being Flambert's BIBLIOMANIA (1929) written in 1836, when the author was not fifteen years old!

These books are not tools and have no reference value to the collector. They do emphasize, however, the interest that has been continually maintained in bibliography and collecting and will give one an hour or so of very pleasant reading. These and similar items are examples of the true bookman's zeal for his hobby. The best of materials went into the physical production of these books, and the whole job was purely a labor of love on Dr. Koch's part.

Lang, Andrew (1844-1912)

> THE LIBRARY, with a Chapter on Modern English Illustrated Books by Austin Dobson. 8vo., blue cloth, numerous plates and woodcuts. First edition, London, 1881.
> $7.50
>
> The same. Large paper, one of 300 copies, buckram with gold title and ornament, uncut, 8vo. Second Edition, London and New York, November 1892.
> $10.00
>
> As above. Small paper copy
> $3.00

86

Lang was a prolific writer, being the author of a long list of books on widely dissimilar subjects. He had a half dozen translations to his credit and edited, as well, twenty or more volumes.

Entering Edinburgh Academy at the age of ten, he remained there for six years. He then spent a year at St. Andrew's University, matriculating at Balliol College, Oxford in 1865. He was a fellow of Merton College for eight years and decidedly the product of a thorough classical education.

The chapter titles of Lang's book, namely, "An Apology for the Book Hunter," "The Library," "The Books of the Collector," and "Illustrated Books," are indications of the popularity of the book when first issued and of its continued interest to bookmen of the present day. It is a delightful example of a book about books and can be read with considerable entertainment and profit.

Lang brings to his readers all of the classical subjects perpetually dear, it would seem, to the heart of collectors. Bibliography, Book-hunting, Bookstalls, Booksellers, Bookcases, Libraries, Manuscripts, Early Printed Books, Uncut Copies, Books on Vellum, First Editions, and Fashions in Book Collecting are but a few of the hundreds of subjects he treats in detail.

The late Mr. Lang was an honest gentleman, for he remarks in his preface to the above second edition:

"The taste for large paper copies of new books has greatly increased since THE LIBRARY was written. It does not become an author to complain whose own modest gains are increased by this fashion. But it seems clear enough that the fashion . . . is exaggerated. It is not every book, by any means, that is the better for being printed on large paper."

It is possible that present day collectors who went through the Limited Edition craze of a few years back might not have been so severely "burned" had they but read Mr. Lang's observations of forty years ago! Tall copies and limited editions were being printed long before the time of Mr. Lang, and doubtless the practice will continue for long after our own day.

Lang, Andrew (1844-1912)

BOOKS AND BOOKMEN. 8vo, original half cloth, paper label, gilt top, uncut, illustrated. First issue of the first edition, Longmans, London, 1887.

$10.00

Of this book, it has been recorded that a copy in the Gross Library contained on its fly leaf the following note, "This is the original edition published in

January, 1877, the greater part of which was immediately called in, that the article on Parish Registers might be cancelled. In this form, therefore, the book is extremely rare."

A nice, though perhaps minor, little bibliographical problem would appear to exist in connection with this work, for there is also a copy bound in blue cloth, with gold title bearing the publication place and date of New York, 1866, a year earlier than that of the above described London edition. The American copy can usually be obtained for $5.00. There were also published of this American edition 100 copies on large paper; copies of this have sold for $7.50. In 1892, another edition was issued in New York and London.

Lang is a good essayist and writes interestingly on a variety of bookish topics in this particular volume.

Lone, Emma Miriam (1872-   )

>SOME NOTEWORTHY FIRSTS IN EUROPE DURING THE FIFTEENTH CENTURY. 425 numbered copies containing 35 illustrations of incunabula, 8vo., cloth. New York, 1930.
>$8.50

Among all the authors of books about books mentioned in this volume, it is with pleasure and a great deal of satisfaction that the names of at least two women can be included. Miss Lone is of course one, and the other, as some readers have already surmised, is Margaret B. Sitwell. It is a coincidence that they are both authorities on incunabula. A work of Miss Sitwell's is described further on in these pages. It is unfortunate that so few women have become interested in bibliography or book collecting although there are numbers of the sex engaged in public and private libraries whose work, for the most part, is unpublished.

A student of incunabula for many years, Miss Lone was the compiler, in 1927 and 1928 for Lothrop C. Harper, a New York dealer, of a series of catalogues in five parts entitled A SELECTION OF INCUNABULA and describing one thousand volumes. This catalogue takes high rank as a reference work and is also of value including, as it does, the prices asked for the individual items, circa 1927-28. These catalogues definitely established the fact that one does not have to go abroad to find copies of the earliest printed books. The catalogue as a set has in itself become a collector's item and is decidedly scarce.

THE BIO-BIBLIOGRAPHY

In her book, which fulfills a promise Miss Lone made in the final part of Harper's catalogue, she has embodied considerable descriptive material of the earliest printed incunabula. Essential information regarding the monuments of early printing is arranged under the headings: Countries and their Languages, Types, Colophons, Collations, Illustrations, Medicine, Law, Arts and Sciences. Various firsts of incunabula are arranged chronologically.

Lowndes, William Thomas (1798[?]-1843)

THE BIBLIOGRAPHER'S MANUAL OF ENGLISH LITERATURE. 2 vols., 8vo., half morocco, t.e.g. William Pickering, London, 1834.

$15.00

Lowndes, the compiler of this great bibliography was born about 1798 and died prematurely in 1843 at the age of forty-five, poverty stricken and worn out by the intensity of fourteen years spent on his MANUAL and on his other handbooks and guides for the bookman. Unfortunately, Lowndes' effort brought him no fame and little, if any, money. The last ten years of his life were spent as a cataloguer for Bohn, the bookseller, who, fourteen years after Lowndes' death in 1857, brought out the four volume second edition of the MANUAL.

Containing records, however brief they may be, of approximately 10,000 books, this MANUAL comprises the greatest attempt ever made to make available to the general reader, collector and dealer a descriptive record of the outstanding contributions to English literature within the scope of the period it covers, namely, from the invention of printing to 1834. Of course, the prices recorded by Lowndes are sadly out of date and are valuable only from a historical point of view and as a record of their times.

The son of a London bookseller, Lowndes came naturally by his love for books. For a time he engaged in the trade as an active dealer but at twenty-two began the MANUAL for which he will ever be remembered.

Unfortunately, there seems to be a lack of individual enterprise today through which it might be possible to revise and bring up to date the entries concerning the individual books first described by Lowndes, even with the necessary funds assured. The first edition, printed by Pickering, was issued in two and in four volumes in 1834. The second edition, as previously noted, was published by Bohn in 1857. A third edition, revised and extended to six volumes, appeared in 1864. A fourth edition was printed in 1896, and no new edition has appeared since that date.

Lowndes, William Thomas (1798[?]-1843)

THE BRITISH LIBRARIAN, or Book-Collectors Guide to the Formation of a Library in all Branches of Literature, Science and Art, etc. 8vo, half calf, uncut. London, 1839-42.
$12.50

Of this work which was issued in parts in 1839, only eleven were published. Lowndes began the compilation of prices, notes, references and authors at a time in life when he was ill and exceedingly low in finances. The labor of the task together with the mental strain and worry to which he was subjected caused a breakdown from which he never recovered. His projected bibliography, which he intended to extend to twenty-four parts, remains uncompleted.

Lxivmos

LXIVMOS (64 mos.), A News Sheet edited by James D. Henderson, Scrivener. Brookline, Massachusetts, 1927.
Per Year, $3.00

This entertaining News Sheet sponsored by an active real estate man, who is also a famed collector, was published primarily for the collector interested in miniature books; in other words, books not more than four inches in height. The work of publication was carried on by a group of book lovers who were organized by Mr. Wilbur Macy Stone, a noted collector of these little books. The News Sheets of the LXIVMOS, largely through the efforts of Scrivener Henderson, have been printed at a number of famous presses in the United States and Europe.

The publication is replete with reports and descriptions from various libraries and collectors. Readers are recommended for particulars regarding titles and the books collected by members of the LXIVMOS Society to Volume 33, Number 1 of the Bulletin of the New York Public Library for January, 1929, containing an account by R. W. G. Vail of an exhibition of these Lilliputian books.

THE BIO-BIBLIOGRAPHY

MacCutcheon, George Barr (1866-1928)

> BOOKS ONCE WERE MEN, An Essay for Book-lovers, with an introduction by William Dana Orcutt. Limited to 1000 copies. Thin 8vo, boards, cloth back, gilt top. New York, 1931.
>
> $3.50

MacCutcheon, the author of the never-to-be-forgotten romance novels laid in the mythical kingdom of Graustark, and whose first editions are now collectors' items, was, himself, a collector of great note as well as a successful writer. His collections of the work of Dickens and Thackeray were the finest that had ever been brought together. They were sold at auction on April 21 and 22, 1926.

McKerrow, R. B. (1872-   )

> AN INTRODUCTION TO BIBLIOGRAPHY FOR LITERARY STUDENTS. 8vo, cloth. First edition, Clarendon Press, Oxford, 1927.
>
> $6.00

This book originated in 1913 as a paper, NOTES ON BIBLIOGRAPHICAL EVIDENCE FOR LITERARY STUDENTS AND EDITORS OF ENGLISH WORKS OF THE SIXTEENTH AND SEVENTEENTH CENTURIES. Subsequently this became a pamphlet of 102 pages, and now has been expanded into the present volume of 360 pages.

Dr. McKerrow is a master of bibliography and has made his book an interesting comprehensive review and study of the subject. While the author carefully explains that he is not writing for book collectors, yet it behooves every collector who aspires to the distinction of the title, to acquire as early as possible a thorough grounding in the principles of bibliography. McKerrow's is as good a text book for this purpose as one could desire.

While in effect the book lives up to its title, being of interest mainly to the literary student, yet it is of value to any one concerned with old and rare books. The volume covers mainly English book production to about 1800 with special reference to the Shakespearian period, yet it is a handbook neither of printing nor of bibliography. The author describes the various processes of book making and writes entertainingly on a number of questions, such as the format of books, false dates, undated editions, fakes and facsimiles, author's copy, proofs, etc. A discussion of these subjects by a man of McKerrow's scholarship is of importance to the bookman and will be found to contain sources of important conclusions. The Appendix includes among other data a brief sketch of the history of printing; an essay on printing types; a list of Latin place names and a note on Elizabethan handwriting.

Of the many books on printing, this is one of the best, for it is full of curious details which do much to hold the interest of the reader.

The author was educated at Harrow and Trinity College, Cambridge. For a time he lectured in English Literature and Bibliography at King's College of the University of London and for years has been Secretary of the English Bibliographical Society. He is an accepted authority on British Booksellers and Printers to 1640 and has numerous articles of a bibliographical nature to his credit.

McMurtrie, Douglas (1888-   )

> THE GOLDEN BOOK, The Story of Fine Books and Bookmaking Past and Present. Finely illustrated, large 8vo, designed cloth. Chicago, 1927.
>
> $6.00

This is a splendid book on printing by one who is an authority on the subject and provides an excellent item for the young collector to read as a part of his education. It is a popular history, rather than a work for the more experienced bookman.

McMurtrie takes his readers back to the early days of Egyptian hieroglyphics and winds up with Mr. F. W. Goudy, the well-known modern printer. It is a far cry between the time represented in the beginning of the book and its end, yet the entire period is adequately covered, and one becomes impressed with the progress the printed book has made and its importance to the world.

In addition to the above copy there was a limited edition of 220 in special binding signed by the author and containing three extra illustrations.

Morley, Christopher (1890-   )

> EX LIBRIS CARISSIMIS. 8vo, boards, cloth back, gold title, limited to 1000 copies. University of Pennsylvania Press, Philadelphia, 1932.
>
> $2.00

The books of Christopher Morley have long enjoyed the distinction of being collected. This book in consequence has double value for those who believe that Morley's writings will last. Not only has the author provided his fans with another item for their collection but he has made them happy by writing of subjects in which most of his readers have a natural interest.

In 1930 Dr. A. S. W. Rosenbach established at the University of Pennsylvania the chair of Fellowship in Bibliography, and Mr. Morley was the first to fill the office. His five lectures, being in the main informal talks on books and the personalities behind them, constitute the text of this little volume. Morley secures the respect of the trade and the collector alike by not attempting to discuss bibliography or collecting from the standpoint of an authority. Rather, he brings to the reader's attention the books and authors that have for him a sincere personal appeal.

Newton, A. Edward (1863-   )

> THE AMENITIES OF BOOK COLLECTING. Illustrated, one plate in color. 8vo, boards, gilt top, uncut. First Edition with inserted slip at p. 268, scarce, Boston, 1918.
> $75.00

Probably no other book on the subject has been published for many years back which met with such success or attracted so much popular attention to book collecting as did Newton's AMENITIES. It is a fascinating and illuminating story. The reader is given a hearty taste of the good work that Newton came to do in succeeding years for the hobby of book collecting which so gripped his heart and mind.

As one of the most active of modern collectors, with the necessary funds and such leisure as he could snatch from his manufacturing business, Newton has done much to arouse a tremendous interest in fine and rare books. He has since written and had published a goodly number of other books, all pertaining directly to collecting or at least with a bookish flavor. Many of his readers feel, however, that he has yet to equal his first effort.

A. Edward Newton is as near a perfect example of a business man turned bookman as one would want to write about. Interested since boyhood in collecting books he had the courage which so many other business men have lacked to turn away from his active commercial interests while still in the prime of life and devote himself wholly to his hobby of collecting.

Reaching the post of Chairman of the Board of the Cutter Electrical Manufacturing Company, which he took over in 1895 in a bankrupt condition, Newton has behind him a successful and prosperous business career. He brings now to his collecting and to the founding of his extensive library at Oak Knoll, in Dalesford, Pennsylvania, the same courage that enabled him to accumulate the funds which have made it possible for him to enjoy his pastime to the utmost.

As the reader of this first book of Newton's may surmise, he is a great Johnsonian. His collection of the works of Doctor Samuel Johnson is exceeded only by those in the Adam Library in Buffalo. One of his recent acquisitions is the sale catalogue of Doctor Johnson's library. This was presented to Newton by Victor Rothchild of London. There is only one other known copy, that being in the British Museum. Much of the literary and collecting interest in Johnson and his contemporaries that has been manifest in recent years is directly due to Newton. While the ramifications of his collecting activities are today many and varied, in the pursuit of his Johnson books he followed a first principle of collecting in that he stuck carefully to the works of a single author.

THE AMENITIES OF BOOK COLLECTING has run through five editions and will undoubtedly be reprinted again and again. Probably 20,000 copies have been sold to date. This is a large number for a work upon such a specialized subject. While one may not be able to own the first edition, a copy of the book should be upon every collector's shelves. The writer paid $12 for his first edition. The book brought $145 at an auction in May 1930.

Newton, A. Edward (1863-   )

A MAGNIFICENT FARCE, and Other Diversions of a Book Collector. 8vo, boards. Boston, 1921.

$7.50

Newton frequently refers to himself as a "scissors and paste" writer, giving the far from true impression that he is a compiler of books rather than an original writer. No one, however, who can tell a story with his charm and ingenuity or who can rewrite literary history with his sense of restraint and effect need be concerned over his reputation as a *littérateur* and author in his own right. This particular volume is one more book for the collector to include in his working library. Newton covers his customary wide range. Between chapters dealing with "A Quarto Hamlet" and "A Sane View of Walt Whitman," there are articles pertaining to international politics and the economics of bookselling.

Newton, A. Edward (1863-   )

> THIS BOOK COLLECTING GAME. 8vo, boards, cloth back, paper label, gilt top, numerous illustrations in full color and in aquatone, large paper. Limited Edition, signed by the author, boxed. Boston, 1928.
> $30.00
> Trade Edition, Boston, 1928. $10.00

Mr. Newton is a great humanist and this trait together with his amusing philosophy and intimate manner with his readers makes his books a delight to the collector. Newton's own library provided the illustrations for many of the rare books described in the pages of this volume. As a commentator on all that pertains to rare books, Newton, as has often been said, is without a peer in our time. He discusses first edition peculiarities and tells many delightful personal stories of his experiences in England and America.

The outstanding feature of this book is the inclusion of his now famous list of "One Hundred Good Novels to Collect." This has since been widely quoted. Book dealers in particular have paid attention to this list which for a time at least was productive of much business for them. The list is arranged alphabetically by title and is interesting because of the variety and types of books suggested. TOM JONES and PAMELA become companions for MCTEAGUE by Norris and THE THREE BLACK PENNIES by Hergesheimer.

Northrup, Clark S. (1872-   )

> A REGISTER OF BIBLIOGRAPHIES OF THE ENGLISH LANGUAGE AND LITERATURE, with contributions by J. Q. Adams and A. Kenogh. Royal 8vo, cloth, 750 copies by the Yale University Press, New Haven, 1925.
> $5.00

This is one of the handiest and most useful books in the reference library of the writer. No matter what subject the collector is interested in, he will find in this single volume an excellent working bibliography. Sabin's BIBLIOGRAPHY OF BIBLIOGRAPHIES, 1875; the contribution to the subject by Stein published in Paris in 1897; and that of the John Crerar Library of Chicago in 1900; together with Courtney's English, three volume REGISTER OF NATIONAL BIBLIOGRAPHY, 1905-12, have all served their purpose and paved the way for this work of

Northrup's. It contains a tremendous amount of bibliographical data. Furthermore, the contents are presented in such an interesting manner that even the casual reader will find much of interest.

A list of general reference books on bibliographical matters is included. Professor Joseph G. Adam and Professor Andrew Kenogh also contributed to the work some valuable additions to the existing bibliographies of the drama and the Elizabethan authors. There is an excellent index.

In the thoroughness with which the work has been compiled, the book is beyond criticism. Many of the bibliographies that Professor Northrup has included may seem of minor importance but many times it is from just such references that the collector, librarian, dealer or research worker is able to find the exact material he is seeking.

Orcutt, William Dana (1875-   )

IN QUEST OF THE PERFECT BOOK, Reminiscences and Reflections of a Bookman. 8vo, boards, decorated cloth and dust wrapper, gilt top. Trade Edition, Boston, 1926.

$5.00

Printed in Lanston Monotype Fournier on Warren's Olde Style wove paper, and with many illustrations, this is a beautiful addition to the literature of books about books. It is a volume of intimate and companionable nature that will strike many a responsive chord in the hearts of its readers. Orcutt has, perhaps, repeated much that has been told before, but he has done it in an earnest and interesting way and of books of this type there can, as George H. Sargent said, "never be too many."

A large paper edition of 365 copies autographed by the author, with additional illustrations, two of which are in color, was also printed. This was bound in half boards with a vellum back, gilt top and boxed. This edition was priced at fifteen dollars on publication.

Orcutt, William Dana (1875-   )

MASTER MAKERS OF THE BOOK, Being a Consecutive Story of the Book from a Century before the Invention of Printing Through the Era of the Dove's Press. 12mo, cloth, frontispiece. New York, 1928.

$2.50

THE BIO-BIBLIOGRAPHY

Orcutt, with his usual modesty and charm, presents for the reader of this volume a history of the evolution of the book from a century before the invention of printing through the era of the Doves Press. This printing house, incidentally, was established in 1900 by Emery Walker with capital provided by Mrs. Cobden-Sanderson. It enjoyed a life of sixteen years. The purpose of the author in preparing this book was to reveal to the reader the progressive steps in the evolution of printing and to describe as well the men who were responsible for the development of the book from the earliest days.

The biographical descriptions of the great printers which one sees, through his written word, working through various political and social changes, make them seem very real and alive. One is better able to understand their personalities and the significance and effect upon their own and later times of the books they produce.

Crediting Francis Petrarch, born near Avignon in 1304, with being one of the forerunners of Aldus in the origin and evolution of printing, Orcutt in a brief review of his life states that Petrarch, while studying law at Bologna, made his first collection of books, "finding the lure of the collector far more important than the demands of legal knowledge."

Like many other book collectors that were to follow him, down even to the present day Petrarch received scant encouragement from his family, in fact, none at all, for his father, on discovering his son's neglect of his legal studies for the joys of book collecting, promptly burned his precious manuscript volumes, and undoubtedly would have at once destroyed Petrarch's small but important library had not the youth promised to devote himself to his legal studies.

Then as now, however, bibliomania was a most insidious disease, for, try as he would, Petrarch could not live up to his promise. "The attractions of the written word proved irresistible." Petrarch declared that he had become afflicted with the "writing disease" and that "daily the disease becomes more virulent."

MASTER MAKERS will provide, particularly for the new collector, an easy introduction to the history of typography. It is a real contribution to the literature of bibliography and printing.

William Dana Orcutt is a distinguished bibliophile who knows his subject of book history thoroughly. None of his books are to be considered in the light of reference works, but they are delightful additions to any bookman's working library. The author endeavors constantly to brighten his array of facts with

BOOKS ABOUT BOOKS

biographical details of famous printers. His books abound with the romance that can usually be found in connection with the development of any new art.

Orcutt, William Dana (1875-   )

> THE BOOK IN ITALY DURING THE FIFTEENTH AND SIXTEENTH CENTURIES, Facsimile reproductions of the Most Famous Printed Volumes, Introduction by Guide Biagi. Large paper, limited to 750 copies. New York, 1928.
> $12.50

Henry L. Mencken in reviewing this book would undoubtedly remark that it lacks an index. While an index to a book of this type would be a most useful adjunct, yet this oversight can be forgiven in view of the beautiful work that Orcutt has produced. Its fine printing, format, plates and typography are a great credit to his care and judgment.

Entirely apart from the value of this volume as an introduction for the student to early Italian typography, the reader becomes acquainted, even though briefly, with the Laurentian Library at Florence and its world renowned librarian, the late Dr. Guide Biagi, who was also custodian of the Medici, the Michelangelo, and the de Vinci archives. Facing page fourteen of Orcutt's IN QUEST OF THE PERFECT BOOK, is a magnificent photograph of this great student of early printing, and the accompanying text gives a brief description of the man and his interests.

The average young reader of THE BOOK IN ITALY can probably never know personally any of the great librarians, bookmen or collectors of the present day. If he could but meet them, however, it would be found that through their mutual interest in books, even though one were but a student and the other the master, they would be on common ground and a lasting friendship would result.

Orcutt has written feelingly of his meeting with Dr. Biagi saying, "I first saw him there, sitting on a bench in front of one of the carved *plutei* designed by Michelangelo—he greeted me with an old-school courtesy. When he discovered my genuine interest in the books he loved and realized that I came as a student eager to listen to the master's word, his face lighted up and we were at once friends."

Dr. Biagi was indeed Orcutt's teacher, and it is fitting that he above everyone else should have written the introduction to THE BOOK IN ITALY. The result is a lasting credit to both teacher and pupil.

In selecting the material for this book, Orcutt chose 132 pages from 199 selected by Dr. Biagi in 1900 for an exhibit of Italian printing shown at the Paris Exposition. These samples are grouped by cities with an accompanying text to describe how the art came to enter Subiaco, the first city in Italy in which a press was set up. Thence the masters in Venice, Naples, Milan, Florence and other cities are named and the peculiarities of their equipment and technique enumerated.

Twenty-five or thirty years ago no American bookman would have thought of producing a volume of this character. If he had, he could have expected few sales and little or no resulting financial support. Interest in the history of fine printing has developed greatly, however, in recent years although as the majority of book lovers are long on their appreciation for the beautiful, but short on cash, the need is for similar books at less, perhaps, than half the cost of the present volume. This particular work is, of course, of primary interest to the bookman. It and similar ones should be available to students in art and other schools. The value of such works from the standpoint of text books in history, art and the humanistic movement cannot be over estimated.

Osler, Sir William (1849-1919)

INCUNABULA MEDICA, a Study of the Earliest Printed Medical Books, 1467-1840. Portrait and numerous facsimiles, 4to, original boards, buckram back. London, 1923.

$45.00

Number nineteen of the Illustrated Monographs of the Bibliographical Society, this is now one of the scarcest and most difficult to obtain. Osler died at Oxford on December 29, 1919, thus being denied the joy of seeing his work in print. Dr. Harvey S. Cushing in his admirable LIFE, to which the writer is indebted for many pleasant hours, says in volume II, page 394, "Osler's intention to print a complete list of the early medical incunabula led him into difficulties which only the bibliographers of incunabula can appreciate. The task was finally handed over to Mr. Scholderer of the British Museum to complete, and the volume INCUNABULA MEDICA was eventually published by the Bibliographical Society in 1923, nearly four years after Osler's death. It contains a preface by A. W. Pollard; Osler's address as President of the Bibliographical Society and a bibliographical list of 217 books (1467-1840)."

On August 3, 1912, in a letter to Dr. S. Weir Mitchell, Osler mentions this catalogue for the first time, saying, "I have been working at the earliest printed medical books up to 1840 which forms a most interesting group." A year later, almost to a day, on August 25, 1913, he is again writing Mitchell, "I have been studying the earliest printed medical books to 1840 to get a picture of the professional mind of the period. I have traced about 140 and have photographs of the most important. All are thirteenth century Arabic, Salernian, or contemporary. The Greeks had not come into their own—only the aphorisms of Hippocrates and one small tractate of Galen! I shall make it my presidential address at the Bibliographical Society."

Again, on the twentieth of December of the same year, writing to Fielding H. Garrison, Osler indicates that his study of medical incunabula is still close to his heart and the work steadily progressing, "I hope before long," he says, "to print my paper of the early printed books up to 1840 dealing with them as illustrating the minds of the profession during the earlier years of printing. I have been getting some treasures lately." In an early paragraph of his address before the Bibliographical Society, Osler states his own relation to his subject. "Not as an expert bibliographer, but as a representative of an ever increasing group of ordinary book lovers, I have tried in the casual studies of a life devoted to hospital and consulting practice to glean two things, the book biographies of the great men of science, and the influence of their books in promoting the progress of knowledge."

Osler, as Dr. Cushing has pointed out, found relief within the walls of his library from the burden the war placed upon his shoulders. In spite of his many duties and visits to camps and hospitals, he felt that the cataloguing of his books should continue, and he worked harder than ever to complete or at least tie up the loose ends of his many bibliographical ventures. More often than not, without the assistance of a secretary, for in those days, few hands if any could be spared from actual war work, Osler undoubtedly found his task far from easy. He writes in January 1915 to L. L. Marshall, "I am still struggling to finish my paper on the Early Printed Medical Books. It is rather a heavy job."

Early spring finds him still seeking sources of information for his contribution to medical bibliography, for on April 15 he writes again to Garrison, "Would it be possible to let me have a list of your incunabula up to and including 1840? In the list I am preparing I would like to put S.G.L. (Surgeon's General Library) after a good many."

Another year comes round and Osler is still plugging away. On January 12,

1916 to Dr. E. C. Streeter of Boston he says, "I am struggling with my incunabula paper but get very little time for work at it." Again on February 7 to L. L. Mackall he writes, "My early printed books paper hangs fire. I can get very little time for work." March 26 finds Osler again bemoaning the increasing pressure which leaves him no leisure for his bibliographical study, for in a note to Garrison whom he is congratulating on his new HISTORY OF MEDICINE he says, "I wish I could get my list to 1840 finished. I get no time for work, incessant calls of one sort or another." Before the close of the month he again speaks of his unfinished paper, this time to J. J. Walsh, "I am working at the earliest printed medical books."

Apparently, Osler put in some good licks during the summer for on October 5 he is again writing to Garrison, this time on a post card, "My incunabula list partially complete." In response to an earlier communication (April 15) Garrison had sent Osler the list of early printed books in the Surgeon's General Library and Osler goes on to say, "I will put in the S.G.L. Have you any additions since you sent the list?"

On November 17, 1917, there is evidence in a letter to Dr. George Dock, that Osler had surrendered to the technical difficulties encountered and had entrusted his data to Mr. Scholderer of the British Museum. He briefly reports, "My catalogue is under revision at the British Museum. I shall hope to have it out next year."

The final reference to the progress of his bibliography was in a letter dated January, 1918 sent to Captain Archie Mallock, but it adds nothing new to the history of his paper for he simply says, "The incunabula list is complete and is being revised item by item at the B. M. Pollard would not risk any mistake."

Though he failed through no fault of his own to complete it, Osler started and made possible the eventual publication of an exceedingly valuable reference work in the field of medical incunabula. This was in a distinct sense the forerunner of other bibliographies and lists which have done much to enrich the sources of information that are now at hand for the convenience of the physician and the collector who are interested in the historical background of the medical profession.

Among these later lists may be mentioned the following:

1925 LIST OF OLD MEDICAL BOOKS IN THE POSSESSION OF DR. LE ROY CRUMMER, compiled and printed by Dr. and Mrs. Crummer.
1929 DR. WILLIAM NORTON BULLARD'S COLLECTION OF MEDICAL INCUNABULA.

BOOKS ABOUT BOOKS

1930 CHECK LIST OF MEDICAL INCUNABULA IN THE NEW YORK ACADEMY OF MEDICINE, by Miss Lester Ford.

1931 LIST OF INCUNABULA IN THE COLLEGE OF PHYSICIANS OF PHILADELPHIA, by Charles P. Fisher.

1931 INCUNABULA MEDICA IN THE HENRY HUNTINGTON LIBRARY, by H. R. Mead.

Osler, Sir William (1849-1919)

BIBLIOTHECA OSLERIANA, A Catalogue of Books Illustrating the History of Medicine and Science. Thick 4to, cloth. The Clarendon Press, Oxford, 1929.

$22.50

This exact and authoritative catalogue of the library collected by Sir William Osler, largely arranged and annotated prior to his death, was bequeathed by him to McGill University. It may now be seen in the Strathcoma Medical Building in Montreal, where the books are beautifully housed. Although Osler worked steadily for years on this catalogue, he was unable to complete it, and after his death the task was carried on, and the entire work edited by W. W. Francis, Librarian of the Osler Library; R. H. Hill of the Bodleian Library, whom the writer had the pleasure of meeting in Oxford in 1929 just as the completed catalogue came from the press; and Archibald Mallock, Librarian of the New York Academy of Medicine.

To those who remember Osler the bookman, as well as Osler the physician and teacher, it is easy to appreciate that under the rules laid down many years before his death, the catalogue has proven an indispensable reference book. Not its least valuable section is the copious index which is a guide to the vast number of bibliographical notes descriptive of the 7778 titles that are included.

While this catalogue is naturally of more interest to the advanced collector who specializes in medical and scientific books, yet its Bibliographical Section contains many items which are of interest to the student collector who wishes to know what books to read and acquire at the beginning of his career in order that he may avoid the many pitfalls that are ever open to catch the uninformed buyer. It is, in addition, one of the few library catalogues in which the general reader will find much of interest. Page after page can be read as easily as any well written prose. This is indeed rare in a catalogue, for ordinarily they are hardly more than uninteresting and uninspiring check lists. Perhaps, however, the one best reason for having this catalogue on one's shelf is as a memorial and tribute to Osler himself. As a lover and collector of books and as a man, Sir William had few equals. President for many years of the London Bibliographical Society, a post which he held at his death, Osler did much to promote interest in rare and fine books and to bring about a closer relationship between collector and dealer.

Osler was born in Ontario in 1849. He graduated from the medical course at McGill University in 1872, returning after two years abroad to a lectureship which was shortly followed by his appointment as a full professor. Ten years later, he went to the University of Pennsylvania and after five years became the first Physician in Chief of the then newly founded Johns Hopkins University. After seventeen years in Baltimore, he was appointed in 1905 Regis Professor of Medicine at Oxford University, which high academic seat he held until his death in 1919 at seventy years of age.

There are many biographical tributes to Osler's extraordinarily full and interesting life, but the most complete is Dr. Harvey Cushing's LIFE. A brief but authoritative sketch has been included by Dr. William S. Thayer in his OSLER AND OTHER PAPERS, published by the Johns Hopkins Press of Baltimore in 1931.

Besides Osler's BIBLIOTHECA OSLERIANA which comprised his most important books, he left two other valuable collections. One, chiefly of modern medical works, went to Johns Hopkins, and the other, embracing the field of English Literature which his son Revere would have inherited had he lived, was left to the Tudor and Stuart Club founded at Johns Hopkins in memory of Revere.

An avid collector of books throughout his lifetime, Osler also kept constantly in mind the interests of various school or hospital libraries. He was always buying some choice volume and sending it with his compliments to the individual or institution he knew would most appreciate or had the greatest need of it. These gifts did much to stimulate the formation of many special collections and Osler's unselfish generosity in his book gifts is an example which might well be followed by other collectors.

The system of classification used by Osler in cataloguing his library is entirely original with him. The description of the eight sections in which the books were classified was mentioned in a deed of gift drawn up as early as 1911. These sections are as follows: Bibliotheca Prima, Bibliotheca Secunda, Bibliotheca Litteraria, Bibliotheca Historica, Bibliotheca Biographica, Bibliotheca Bibliographica, Incunabula and Manuscripts. The chief feature of the Osler library and the heart of his catalogue is the Bibliotheca Prima.

BOOKS ABOUT BOOKS

Oswald, John C. (1872-   )

> A HISTORY OF PRINTING, Its development through five hundred years. 8vo, cloth. New York and London, 1928.
>
> $10.00

The most important feature of this book is its summary of the history of printing from the one inch movable type to about the year 1520. This period embraces approximately seventy years from the birth of incunabula or "cradle books." The author is to be commended for his accuracy and the care with which he wrote this book. For the period following 1520, however, any of a number of other authorities may be read with equal success and pleasure. Oswald's real contribution to the history of printing lies within the scope of its relatively first few years, a period in which, it is apparent, he is personally much interested.

This volume is made more interesting by the inclusion of some 140 fine illustrations, of which a number are in color, to picture to the reader the work of many early printers.

Pearson, Edmund L. (1880-1937)

> QUEER BOOKS, with reproductions of illustrations from quaint nineteenth century books. 8vo, cloth. New York, 1928.
>
> $3.00

An interesting work on the literary curiosities of the early nineteenth century, their pruderies and sensationalisms. The author deals with temperance novels, propaganda novels, orations, gift books, annuals, queer poets, chapbooks, broadsides, sensational love stories, murders, and seductions.

Philobiblion, The

> THE PHILOBIBLION, A Monthly Bibliographical Journal, Containing Critical Notices of and Extracts from Rare, Curious, and Valuable Old Books. 8vo, Parts 1 to 111, Vols. 1 and 11, printed on India paper, half morocco, gilt. New York, 1862-3.
>
> $7.50

THE BIO-BIBLIOGRAPHY

Published monthly by the old New York bookselling firm of George P. Philes and Company, this publication is filled with curious items on topics of general information concerned with literature. Notices are included of rare books and library sales. It has the usual "Notes and Queries" section common to most journals of this type. Each volume is well indexed. The catalogues of books offered for sale by the firm are interesting as providing examples of the books that were generally sought after by collectors of the Civil War period.

Pollard, Alfred W. (1859-   )

FINE BOOKS. 8vo, red cloth, gold title and ornaments, large paper. One of the Connoisseurs Library edited by Cyril Davenport. London, 1912.
$12.50

Long classed by dealers as one of the best books about books, this work of Pollard's contains an excellent though brief historical sketch of some of the early book collectors and their influence on collecting from the bibliophiles of the later Roman Empire through the eighteenth century. Much space is devoted to a discussion of book illustrations prior to the introduction of mechanical reproduction. The book is illustrated with forty splendid plates, has a good index and a bibliography of books on collecting, printing, incunabula and general works pertaining to the science of bibliography and collecting. It is particularly for its material on collecting, early printing and bibliography that the book has its greatest appeal. Readers without some previous knowledge of incunabula and early illustrated books may find much of it rather heavy going.

FINE BOOKS should be on every collector's shelves along with Pollard's other contributions to bibliography and book collecting. The book is recommended especially to young student readers as an introduction to the general subject of typography from the invention of printing through the first century of its development. It is a fine companion to his EARLY ILLUSTRATED BOOKS which, in fact, Pollard has enlarged upon in the present volume.

E. Gordon Duff's EARLY PRINTED BOOKS belongs in the same group and should be read in conjunction with Pollard's works.

BOOKS ABOUT BOOKS

Pollard, A. W.; G. R. Redgrave and others

SHORT TITLE CATALOG OF BOOKS PRINTED IN ENGLAND, SCOT-
LAND, AND IRELAND AND OF ENGLISH BOOKS PRINTED ABROAD
1575-1640. 4to, half canvas, boards, limited to 500
copies printed for the Bibliographical Society. London,
1926.

$20.00

Containing 26,130 entries, this is a valuable and much needed work. All known English books from 1475 to 1640 are described by title, size and publisher. Each entry is numbered and arranged in alphabetical order of author's name or heading. Different editions of the same book are in chronological order. Some 150 libraries and individual owners of books are thus registered. In instances of the rare or unique volumes, the home of the copy described is given.

In January, 1927, writing in the *Boston Evening Transcript*, the late George H. Sargent, who for forty years conducted the column devoted to rare books known as "The Bibliographer," called this "one of the most important bibliographical publications of the year, or, for that matter, of many years." This volume might well be a substitute for a large number of reference books and is indispensable to the bibliographer, librarian, student of English Literature, collector or dealer. It is not a catalogue of books known or believed to have been produced but is a register of books of which copies have been traced in stated libraries and collections.

Power, John (1820-1872)

A HANDY BOOK ABOUT BOOKS, for Book-Lovers, Book-Buyers
and Book-Sellers. 8 plates of facsimiles, 8vo., decorative boards, t.e.g. London, 1870.

$12.50

Part I of this volume was enlarged in 1877 by Joseph Sabin of New York to "four times the extent of Power's list" and published as A BIBLIOGRAPHY OF BIBLIOGRAPHIES or, A HANDY BOOK ABOUT BOOKS WHICH RELATE TO BOOKS.

Power divided his book into nine parts including an interesting Appendix and a useful Index. The principal sections relate to Bibliography Chronology which connects the important events associated with the progress of printing and its relation to the development of literature, and Useful Receipts, which gives the customary receipts for the repair and care of books. In addition, there are chapters entitled Typographical Gazetteer or An Outline of History; Booksellers Directory, now, of course, far out of date; and Miscellany and Dictionary of Terms, the latter two chapters being of no small value to the current bookman.

This volume has stamped upon the front and back covers in colors a curious imitation Grolier design. It was, undoubtedly, a popular work in its day and still deserves a place in the bookman's library.

Publishers' Weekly

> PUBLISHERS' WEEKLY, The American Book-Trade Journal. January 1872 to date. R. R. Bowker Company, New York.
>
> Per year, $5.00

In 1872 the AMERICAN LITERARY GAZETTE AND PUBLISHERS' CIRCULAR was incorporated with the PUBLISHERS' WEEKLY. It has become the leading publication of the book trade. This Journal lists, with descriptive notes, all American book publications. It also publishes quarterly announcements of forthcoming books. One of its chief features is its "Books Wanted" section in which dealers and collectors may list their desiderata or books they may wish to sell. A page or more is devoted to a discussion of "Rare Book Notes" and the principal current writers on topics of interest to the bookman are regular contributors to its pages. In short, the PUBLISHERS' WEEKLY provides the medium through which the collector may keep abreast of the tide of literature. It constitutes a most valuable tool well within the reach of all who profess an interest in books.

Ransom, Will

> PRIVATE PRESSES AND THEIR BOOKS. Large 8vo, brown cloth, gold title, limited to 1200 copies. First edition, New York, 1929.
>
> $12.50

For information pertaining to private presses and the books they have issued, Mr. Ransom is the authority for the collector to consult. He has been very thorough in his compilation, having traced three hundred and twenty-five American and European presses which represent two thousand eight hundred and fifty published books.

BOOKS ABOUT BOOKS

While there may be some difference of opinion among collectors as to the ultimate value and worth of books issued in limited editions by private presses, there are many individual volumes which will always command the attention and respect of the book lover. If one is undecided where to begin his collecting career, he might well consider certain books issued by the Kelmscott, Doves, Golden Cockerel, Daniel and Village presses, that have been designed by men such as D. B. Updike, Bruce Rogers, William Edwin Rudge, Edwin Grabhorn, W. A. Dwiggins and Elmer Adler, all of whom are recognized among the foremost book designers of their time.

Any well printed and attractive book issued by a private press should be a welcome addition to a collector's shelves, particularly for the book lover who takes pleasure in looking at and handling a beautiful example of the designer's and printer's skill. While the writer, from a collector's point of view, sticks pretty closely to his particular hobby of books about books, yet some of the items he enjoys most and values highly are representative private press items.

Roberts, W. P. (1862-   )

> THE BOOK HUNTER IN LONDON, Historical and other Studies of Collectors and Collecting. Numerous illustrations, 8vo, cloth. London, 1895.
>
> $7.50

As Roberts says, this book was the outcome of material which had been accumulating for many years past and also of a long and pleasant intercourse with the leading collectors and booksellers of his time in London. Furthermore, it would rightly seem that his own vigorous and constant pursuit of the hobby of book collecting should have qualified him to write entertainingly of his experiences. Roberts gives a brief review of the principle bibliopoles, bibliopolies and bibliomaniacs of the nineteenth century, and his book abounds as well in facts and curious anecdotes relative to "Book Auctions and Sales," "Bookstalls," and "Book-Hunting Localities." The work contains a large amount of well arranged information of interest to the ordinary reader as well as to the confirmed collector.

The first book auction in London took place in 1676 and was conducted by a bookseller of considerable learning named William Cooper. Roberts writes entertainingly of similar high spots in the history of bookselling and collecting, and his pages abound in innumerable stories relative to the localities where rare books were once found.

Further chapters give some account of women as book collectors, and Roberts does not report altogether favorably on them. In addition, he writes of his contemporary collectors, of their special hobbies, of the mistakes that appear in catalogues, of auction sales and of book thieves.

Rogers, Walter T. (1841-1912)

A MANUAL OF BIBLIOGRAPHY, Being an Introduction To The Knowledge Of Books, Library Management And The Art of Cataloguing. Colored frontispiece and 37 other illustrations. Paper, gold title and ornament, t.e.g., uncut, 8vo. New York, 1891.

$5.00

Comprising brief chapters on printing, the development and ornamentations of the book, and upon library economy, this volume also includes a reference bibliography, glossary and index.

The reader will probably be most interested in the library chapter and, of course, in the dictionary of terms in order to further increase his vocabulary of the bookman's language. Rogers' remarks on bibliography and cataloguing definitely date the book and enable even the amateur to appreciate the strides made in these fields in the past forty years.

Rosenbach, A. S. W. (1876-   )

AN AMERICAN JEWISH BIBLIOGRAPHY, Being a List of Books and Pamphlets by Jews or relating to them printed in the United States from the Establishment of the Press in the Colonies until 1850. 8vo, cloth. Number 30 of the publications of the Jewish Historical Society, Baltimore, 1926.

$10.00

In his introduction, Dr. Rosenbach outlines the history of the teaching of the Hebrew language in America; the story of Jewish civic and religious life in the United States in the eighteenth and early nineteenth centuries; the participation of the Jews in the opening of the Ohio and Illinois country; the beginning of the synagogues, Sunday schools and charitable organizations; the genesis of the Reform movement, the missionaries and the converts to and from Judaism; early Jewish authors and dramatists; the theory of the Jewish origin of the American Indian; the participation of American Jews in the early Zionist movement; the massacres in the East; the expeditions to the River Jordan and the constitutions and by-laws of early Jewish congregations and educational societies.

These subjects offer rich fields for the collector and historian, and this bibliographical contribution will do valuable service in indicating the way to sources of accurate information. As might be expected, this bibliography has been prefaced with the usual care and thoroughness that is characteristic of all of Dr. Rosenbach's writings. Being the only list of its kind, this volume is naturally of great assistance to the collector of Jewish literature. It is to be hoped that someone will continue the work and give collectors an additional summary of Jewish bibliography during the last half of the last century. Dr. Rosenbach has attempted to locate all the existing copies of the 700 odd titles he mentions, and he includes in his book many interesting facsimiles as well as a good index.

Rosenbach, A. S. W. (1876-   )

BOOKS AND BIDDERS, The Adventures of a Bibliophile. Illustrated, 8vo, cloth, limited edition, one of 785 copies signed by the author. Boston, 1927.

$35.00

Originally read by collectors in the form of papers contributed to the *Saturday Evening Post*, these entertaining essays have served to bring Dr. Rosenbach closer to the collector than he had ever been before. Long known as "the world's greatest book dealer," and selling in the main only to the class of wealthy collectors who could afford to pay the prices at which he valued his items, Rosenbach, as a dealer to whom the collector with a modest purse might talk, was simply non-existent. Only the elect are admitted to his book-rooms in New York and Philadelphia. It would be sacrilege to call his places of business bookshops!

Being in the trade, Dr. Rosenbach naturally emphasises the commercial aspects of book collecting, yet at the same time, he gives much earnest advice to the collector and writes entertainingly of a variety of subjects connected with his experiences as a seller of rare books to some of the country's most noted collectors. Rosenbach is himself a collector of note as is witnessed by his chapter and later works on children's books.

THE BIO-BIBLIOGRAPHY

Taking George Smith's place as the most successful rare book dealer of his day, Rosenbach is well equipped to tell, with a wealth of anecdote, of his experiences as a dealer and collector. Rosenbach buys to sell again, but he also has the true collector's dislike of parting with his treasures to such an extent that his personal library shelves are filled with items that, but for sentiment and love of books, he could dispose of for what would be a considerable fortune.

Rosenbach's book is naturally largely autobiographical, and if at times he seems biased in his opinions, it must be remembered that one is reading of the experiences of a man who, for many years, has been able by wholesale purchase and a willingness to pay what amounts almost to unheard of prices to outbid with ease other hopeful buyers at London and American auctions. The man Rosenbach is literally in a class by himself. Any runner-up who succumbs to his rapid fire actions in acquiring the books he is bidding for can but admire his courage and respect the knowledge and scholarship that enables him to recognize the great representative items of the world's literature, many of which are passed over with hardly a glance by other less informed dealers.

That Rosenbach is appreciative of the worth of true bibliographical knowledge and is desirous of making available to students some source of inspiration which may engender a love of literature and fine books, is shown by his gift in 1930 to the University of Pennsylvania of $20,000 for the establishment of an honorary fellowship in bibliography.

Rosenbach, A. S. W. (1876-   )

EARLY CHILDREN'S BOOKS, with bibliographical descriptions of the books in his private collection, Foreword by A. Edward Newton. Illustrated, small folio, half morocco, decorated boards, limited to 585 signed copies, boxed. Portland, 1933.
$25.00

Dr. Rosenbach has long been known among his intimates as a collector of early American children's books, being the owner of what is probably the most outstanding collection. His hobby has finally culminated in the publication of this volume. This particular collection represents far more than the lifetime devotion of a single individual, for Rosenbach's uncle, Moses Polock, like his illustrious nephew a bookseller of more than ordinary note, began the collection

BOOKS ABOUT BOOKS

which, at his death in 1908, came into the hands of the Doctor. Since that time, it has been added to until now 816 volumes are included in the number of titles described by Dr. Rosenbach.

EARLY CHILDREN'S BOOKS is a delightful example of good printing and binding and its text enhances the scholarly reputation of the author. The items are arranged chronologically from 1636 to 1836. The book is of value to the collector of juveniles and belongs in any library of books about books. In addition, its charming preface by Mr. Newton makes it a necessary title to include in any collection of Newtonina.

In addition to this edition of 585 copies, 88 copies of a Special Edition were published at $120 each.

Sabin, Joseph (1821-1881)

> A DICTIONARY OF BOOKS RELATING TO AMERICA, from its Discovery to the Present Time. Bibliographical Society of America, New York, 1868 to date. In parts, each $4.00

Joseph Sabin, Oxford bookseller and publisher, who began this monumental DICTIONARY, was born in England in 1812 and died in the United States in 1881. Thirty-three years of his life were spent in America, where for the most part he was engaged in bookselling. Sabin began his DICTIONARY in 1867 and lived to see eighty-two parts completed. Sometime prior to his death, in fact during the early days of the work, Mr. Wilberforce Eames, the eminent bibliographer, became an assistant to Sabin without pay. On Sabin's death Mr. Eames carried on alone the difficult task of compiling and editing the work. Such funds as were on hand eventually became exhausted and Mr. Eames found himself unable to continue. In 1924 through the efforts of the Library Journal and the generosity of Mr. Joseph Sabin II, the DICTIONARY took on a new lease of life. Later the Bibliographical Society of America undertook its sponsorship and circularized its members and others for additional subscriptions. Since that time the responsibility of the undertaking has rested on the capable shoulders of Mr. R. W. G. Vail and Mr. H. M. Lydenberg. Originally 100 sets on large paper and 500 sets on ordinary paper were printed. The work progressed as rapidly as funds became available and was completed in 1937.

Sabin's purpose which those who followed after him have religiously preserved was to include all notable books, pamphlets and periodicals written about America or by American authors. The arrangement is alphabetical by authors, anonymous items being entered under their titles. Of each item included is supplied its full title, place, publisher, date, paging, format, notes, and in most instances the names of libraries possessing copies.

This DICTIONARY is one of two great American bibliographical enterprises, the other being Evan's AMERICAN BIBLIOGRAPHY. Although both publications have suffered various delays, their sponsors, despite the death of Mr. Evans in 1935, have shown courage and great industry in their determination to complete and have in print these great master bibliographies. The chief differences between Sabin and Evans is that Sabin includes all notable works which were written by Americans or relate to America no matter where they were printed, while Evans includes only such books as were actually printed in America. Sabin's record is arranged alphabetically by authors, while the items described by Evans are listed chronologically in the order of printing.

Sargent, George H. (1867-1931)

THE WRITINGS OF A. EDWARD NEWTON, A Bibliography. With cogitations by Christopher Morley. 4to, boards linen back, gilt top, uncut, limited to 110 copies. Philadelphia, 1927.

$25.00

As a bookman and particularly as a critic and writer about the books of others, George H. Sargent undoubtedly enjoyed great satisfaction in compiling this bibliography of Newton. The work is accurate, interesting and necessary to those who would collect Newton's books. As a bibliography it has few of the omissions and most of the merits that constitute a really good job. It is attractively printed and bound by the Rumford Press of Concord, New Hampshire and contains to the date of its publication all known items of Newton's, no matter how insignificant.

Morley's comments are illustrative of this popular writer at his best, while Sargent's own introduction is exactly what it should be for a work of this nature in which the published writings of a collector of Newton's appeal are set down.

BOOKS ABOUT BOOKS

Sargent, George H. (1867-1931)

A BUSTED BIBLIOPHILE AND HIS BOOKS, Illustrated. Being a Most Delectable History of the Diverting Adventures of that Renowned Book-Collector, A. Edward Newton. The First and only Edition with all the Original Errours. Paper label, cloth back, original marbled boards, 8vo, 49 pp., uncut, limited to 600 copies. Boston, 1928.
$25.00

The late George H. Sargent, who for years contributed a weekly column to the *Boston Evening Transcript* known as "The Bibliographer," which was replete with items of interest to the book-collector, did an excellent piece of work in providing collectors with his interesting sketch of Mr. A. Edward Newton of Oak Knoll, Dalesford, Pennsylvania and his remarkable library.

Newton is the most popular writer of books about books since the time of Dibdin, who was really responsible in 1806 or thereabouts for the spread of the disease bibliomania which, prior to his time, while known, was kept somewhat under control. Dibdin has had his imitators in Hazlitt, Slater, Burton, Clark, Plomer, Duff, Pollard, Arnold, Roberts, Jackson, Johnson and even Orcutt and Winterich, but no one has been more to blame for fanning a smouldering fire into a holocaust and causing a new epidemic of bibliomania than A. Edward Newton.

Book dealers especially should be grateful for the boom in the rare and second-hand book market which Newton's writings brought about. They should even give him such books as he requires, or at least a life interest in them, which, incidentally, would probably not interest him in the least, as a slight token of their esteem and appreciation. Incidentally, while George H. Sargent did his part in this little volume to immortalize the name of A. Edward Newton, we must not forget Mr. Ellery Sedgwick of Boston, editor of the famed *Atlantic Monthly*, for it was he who first recognized the merits of Mr. Newton's manuscripts and caused them to be published!

All collectors should own and read all of Newton's books. Even the dealers read them to find out what is going on in their own business. The collector should read them for pleasure, inspiration and information. The writer's copy of this particular Newton item, which for him has twice its ordinary value simply because George H. Sargent wrote it, was bought in the Chicago Union

THE BIO-BIBLIOGRAPHY

Station for $4.50 and is now currently priced in dealer's catalogues at $25.00. A nice paper profit? Perhaps, but the writer does not, as a rule, buy books to sell later at a profit and because of Sargent's authorship and the writer's personal knowledge of his lovable characteristics, A BUSTED BIBLIOPHILE AND HIS BOOKS has a very strong sentimental and association value which could not by any means be exchanged for any sum remotely approaching twenty-five dollars.

Facing page fourteen in this book is a photograph of Newton's library. It alone is worth the price of the book and is enough to incite the envy of a saint. Of course, the walls of this beautiful room are lined with books, and Mr. Newton should make its existence in perpetuity possible if only to show to generations yet to come what a gentleman's book-room in his time and country was like. One cannot help but wonder what disposition he will make of his books. Their disbursement at an auction would, it is true, give other collectors a chance to secure many rarities and enable Newton from his grave to enjoy a certain posthumous sporting pleasure in the resulting bidding. Nevertheless the true bookman's heart involuntarily shudders at the prospect of seeing any other book lover's collection scattered again to four score or more collectors after one alone has spent a lifetime, let alone a fortune, in acquiring it.

In the writing of no other bio-bibliographical sketch has the writer taken so much pleasure as in the preparation of the essential facts of Sargent's life.

A descendant of a William Sargent who came to Ipswich, Massachusetts in 1630, George Henry Sargent was born in 1867 and passed away at his Elm Farm in Warren, New Hampshire in 1931. Throughout his life, he was a newspaper man and was proud of his membership in the Fourth Estate. He began his career in St. Paul, Minnesota, as a reporter. He was a sincere, kindly man. Having no books for sale and no axe to grind, Sargent wrote frankly of the aspects and tendencies of collecting as the current news of the subject came to his attention. It is earnestly hoped that some capable editor will compile Sargent's writings in order that they may be readily available to collectors as well as to students of bibliography, for each in his separate field will find in Sargent much of the information as well as inspiration that he will need.

In 1913, he inaugurated his famous column, "The Bibliographer," and without it, the book section of the *Boston Evening Transcript* has never been the same. It is interesting to note that to date no other writer has carried on in the columns of the *Transcript* a discussion of the various phases of book collecting. Sargent's place remains unfilled. No one could, in fact, take his place.

Sargent was a recognized authority of bibliography and probably the most widely quoted for in addition to his *Transcript* articles, he wrote continually, over a period embracing some three decades, for book collecting and bibliographical journals throughout England and the Continent.

For an extended biography of Sargent, the reader is referred to Karl Schriftgresser's splendid tribute which appeared in the March 1931 number of THE BOOKMAN. Another satisfying biography has been written by Charles F. Heartman and appeared in the catalogue of Sargent's library which was sold at auction by Heartman at Metuchen, New Jersey, on December 19, 1931.

Sargent owned, in eighty-three items, the best A. Edward Newton collection in the country, and these books were catalogued separately and sold at auction on the same day. It is well to know that this section of Sargent's library, together with certain other books, was privately purchased and presented en bloc to the New York Public Library where it may be seen and used by all who are interested in book collecting.

In addition to the books by Newton himself, this volume of Sargent's and such other of his writings as can be obtained should be owned by the reader. Heartman's catalogues of the Sargent sale should also be secured. They constitute real collector's items. The catalogue of Sargent's library comprising 247 items aside from his Newton collection is of interest in its revelation of the kind of books a man of Sargent's taste and knowledge should wish to own and make a part of his life and work.

Savage, James

>THE LIBRARIAN. Half calf, 2 plates, 8vo, 3 vols. in 1. London, 1808-9.
>
>$7.50

THE LIBRARIAN was a monthly literary and bibliographical journal of excellent quality which gave an account of scarce, valuable and useful English books.

Sawyer, Charles S. and Darton, F. S.

>ENGLISH BOOKS 1475-1640, A Signpost for Collectors. 100 illustrations, 2 vols., large 8vo, buckram, gilt tops. First edition, London, 1927.
>
>$12.00

THE BIO-BIBLIOGRAPHY

This is one of the best guides ever written to the collecting of English books, and its title could hardly be more descriptive of the purpose which the authors had in mind. They have not emphasized the monetary profits of book collecting as have so many writers. Neither have they boasted of the books in their own libraries or attempted to arouse the envy of the reader by mentioning the great luck of other collectors in picking up for five dollars an item which was subsequently sold for five thousand.

While not exactly a book for the beginner, ENGLISH BOOKS would do much towards giving the young collector something more of a foundation upon which to build his book buying activities than he is usually fortunate enough to possess. It will show the collector that money value is by no means the ultimate end in the consideration of book rarities, dealers to the contrary notwithstanding. The book is very readable and of practical use, covering as it does a wide field in English literature. The authors have described many desirable books and have given the reasons for the position these books occupy.

Before attempting to master this work of Sawyer and Darton, the reader is advised, unless he is experienced, to assimilate first some of the simpler guides to the art and practice of book collecting. The authors have not written with the beginner in mind but rather have produced a scholarly treatise of much valuable information for those who have reached, in their collecting activities, the point of accumulating the real gems of English literature during the period from Chaucer to Galsworthy. Both a plentiful supply of funds as well as expert bibliographical assistance are needed if one's range of activities extend so far. For the collector who comes within this class, however, Sawyer and Darton will provide much of the essential and accurate data necessary for successful guidance, unless one can afford to waste both time and money, in which event one would not be a collector or lover of books but simply a purchaser of merchandise as well as a gambler.

In chronological order, the writers discuss the early English printers, the writers of the Renaissance, the Elizabethans, Shakespeare and the Stuarts, and the writers of the seventeenth century, which will bring to the reader's eye and mind names and a period in literary history with which, perhaps, he is most familiar. It is a pleasure to reiterate and to set down once again the names of Defoe, Pope, Gay, Goldsmith, Gray, Burns, Fielding, Smollett, Swift, Richardson, Cowper, Sterne, and the great Johnson, all of whom and particularly, perhaps, Johnson, did so much to insure for posterity the life and pageantry of their times. In Volume II the Victorians, as exemplified by Dickens and Thackeray, are reached. As Mr. Sawyer is an authority on Dickens, the reader is assured of a careful treatment of the points necessary to the successful collector of Dickens. While only a chapter is devoted to the modern authors, faith is expressed in their work and no concern is shown for the high prices that their first editions are apparently destined to bring.

The first edition of ENGLISH BOOKS consists of 2000 copies printed in Edinburgh for distribution in England and America. The entire edition is uniform in typography, this being, therefore, one of the few modern books about books which has not also been issued in a limited or large paper edition.

Schwarts, Jacob

1100 OBSCURE POINTS, The Bibliographies of twenty-five English and twenty-one American Authors. Royal 8vo, cloth. London, 1931.

$3.50

This volume which includes 550 American and 550 British books is a bibliographical guide of desirable information for collectors and dealers. Dr. Schwarts gives some instructive and little known details of the works of many authors. Among those included are Jane Austin, Robert Browning, Samuel Butler, Lord Byron, James Cabell, Norman Douglas, T. S. Eliot, John Galsworthy, Henry James, D. H. Lawrence, Edgar Allan Poe, Lord Tennyson, Walt Whitman, Oscar Wilde and William Butler Yeats.

Sitwell, Margaret Bingham

INCUNABULA AND AMERICANA 1450-1800, A Key to Bibliographical Study. Royal 8vo, red cloth, gold ornament, t.e.g., decorative end papers. New York, 1931.

$12.50

This is a most excellent guide for the collector or dealer whose activities embrace the field of incunabula. It has the further delightful character of being a fine, substantial book, beautifully printed and bound, and containing a good index.

During her writing of INCUNABULA AND AMERICANA, Miss Sitwell was, as she still is, Librarian of the Annmary Brown Memorial at Providence, Rhode Island.

Not the least valuable part of her volume is the Preface which, in keeping with the prefaces of so many other books by earnest bookmen, is so sincere and grateful for the opportunities that have been made available to the author. In general, prefaces and introductions to books by bookmen contain a rare inspirational quality most helpful to one engaged in any form of research. One might well make and publish a collection of such prefaces, for their reading would do much to dissipate the uncertainties of mind common to all writers who are embarked upon a new road as yet untrod and blocked by haunting fears and questions that shroud in mystery and obscure the passage.

Contrary to most works on the subject of incunabula, Miss Sitwell's book is not beyond the comprehension of the average bookman and collector. As a matter of fact, it serves as a splendid introduction to the study of early printed books.

An extended list of bibliographical reference books is included for the student who would wish to supplement his studies with much collateral reading. The historical chapters give one the necessary background to understand and to acquire a mental picture of the times in which were printed that class of incunabula known as Americana in which Miss Sitwell is so deeply interested. Incidentally, it is Americana in its earliest and most original form. The Reference Section of the book, containing Notes and Definitions, will be found of particular value in furnishing an explanation of the scope of Americana and in supplying the reader with practical details of cataloguing.

The book is divided into three sections: 1. Incunabula (identification, collation, bibliographies); 2. Americana (discovery, colonization, revolution, early printers); 3. Reference Sections (definitions, foreign terms, Latin abbreviations, 15th century place names, woodcuts and bibliographies and monographs of incunabula).

Slater, J. Herbert (1854-1921)

EARLY EDITIONS, A Bibliographical Survey of the Works of Some Popular Modern Authors. Royal 8vo, boards, cloth back, large paper edition limited to fifty copies, signed by the author. London, 1894.
$30.00

In the death of Slater in 1921, collectors throughout the world suffered a keen personal loss. As the founder and editor of BOOK PRICES CURRENT, editor of

BOOKS ABOUT BOOKS

BOOK-LORE, and author of many bibliographical works relating to various phases of book collecting, he exercised a great influence over collectors during his active life.

EARLY EDITIONS was a classic reference work of its day and is still of value to the bookman interested in the period and authors covered. Inquiries regarding its contents addressed to Slater from all parts of the world, brought prompt and complete replies, even though it meant many hours of painstaking research. Slater was not only an English gentleman of the finest type but had as well a sympathetic feeling and regard for his fellow collectors regardless of the phase of their hobby or the country in which they lived.

Slater, J. Herbert (1854-1921)

THE ROMANCE OF BOOK-COLLECTING. 8vo, decorative red cloth, gilt title, frontispiece, uncut. London, 1898.
$5.00
The same. Decorative green cloth. New York, 1898.
$3.00

The writer has recently seen a copy of this book described in an English dealer's catalogue as bound in "original blue buckram" and being the first edition. It was offered at ten shillings, a very reasonable price. Apparently there were at least three bindings in different colors all issued at about the same time. The question of editions is of minor importance in considering this book, however. It is neither a relatively scarce nor expensive book.

The important thing is that the collector add it to his library and to that portion of his shelf space from which he renews at intervals his passion for collecting. This book will likewise play a part in sustaining the aura of romance which surrounds every bibliophile in his quest for books.

Slater writes here in praise of booksellers' catalogues. He compares prices, describes some of his lucky purchases and among other vital chapters describes the London bookshops and their locations of forty years ago. It is a companionable and entertaining volume.

Slater, J. Herbert (1854-1921)

HOW TO COLLECT BOOKS. 8vo, boards, decorative brown cloth, gilt title, t.e.g., illustrated, uncut. First edition, London, 1905.
$5.00

THE BIO-BIBLIOGRAPHY

This is another fine handbook for the collector, especially at the commencement of his career. The various subjects common to most books relating to collecting are discussed in a simple and understandable fashion by Slater. The illustrations are numerous and helpful in explaining the text. There is a good index.

The first two chapters entitled "Hints to Beginners" and "Some Practical Details," together with the eleventh chapter, "Auction Sales and Catalogues," contain a great deal of basic and essential information of value to the young bookman.

In the beginning paragraphs, Slater states the two main divisions of bibliography. The first treats of books with reference to their form, degree of rarity, the history of particular copies or editions and the prices that can be got for them. The second division is concerned with their substance, contents and a critical judgment of their merits. In his text Slater confines himself to the first aspect of bibliography and only incidentally writes upon the subject matter of the second division.

Smith, Harry B. (1860-1936)

> A SENTIMENTAL LIBRARY, Comprising Books Formerly Owned by Famous Writers, Presentation Copies, Manuscripts and Drawings. 56 illustrations, cloth, vellum back, uncut, slip case. Privately printed, 1914.
> $37.50

A dramatic author, who, as Christopher Morley has said, "earned his living writing librettos and spent it buying libraries," Harry B. Smith produced not only a beautiful book but an extraordinary catalogue of his library of books and letters. It is of absorbing interest to the collector of English authors of the seventeenth, eighteenth and nineteenth centuries and will be found most fascinating by the general reader. In it are described the valuable association and presentation copies of books and manuscripts owned by famous writers and collected by Mr. Smith. This library he sold *en bloc* to Dr. A. S. W. Rosenbach, who in turn disposed of the collection to Mr. William B. Elkins. The volume contains a delightful author's Preface and a fine Appreciation by Mr. Luther S. Livingston.

The writer's copy was presented by the author to Mr. William F. Gable and contains with the date, November 10, 1914, the following inscription—

BOOKS ABOUT BOOKS

"If there is anything that a book-collector loves more than acquiring books it is talking about them."

As Smith states in his Preface, it was his purpose to include in this catalogue, "only books which are interesting on account of their associations and books which have been made unique by the addition of letters or manuscripts." "Few," he further states, "have been included merely as rarities or first editions."

Livingston says in his Appreciation that association books are of value "because they bring us, no matter through how many hands they may have passed, into direct communication with the writers."

This work of Smith's is as much a bibliography as a catalogue. Furthermore, it is unsurpassed as a very readable text book covering one of the most interesting periods of English literature. Readers will find within its covers the intimate letters of Byron, Keats, Dickens, Thackeray, Lamb, Shelley, Coleridge, Tennyson, Browning, Rossetti, Carlyle, Johnson, Izaak Walton, and a score of others are represented upon its pages. One is astounded at the variety, the wealth of material that Smith collected.

Unfortunately, the book lacks an index, but as its contents are arranged alphabetically, the section devoted to any one writer is easily found. The book comprises some 332 pages and, aside from its great bibliographical value to the collector, will be of more than passing interest to all bookmen.

Harry B. Smith was also the author of FIRST NIGHTS AND FIRST EDITIONS.

Starret, Vincent (1886-   )

PENNY WISE AND BOOK FOOLISH. Tall 8vo, full brown art boards, gilt, numerous illustrations, slip case, large paper, signed by the author, one of 275 copies. First edition, New York, 1929.

$15.00

Mr. Starret is also the author of A COLLECTOR'S SCRAP BOOK, published in Chicago in 1924, and of numerous magazine articles upon book collecting. He is well known as a Sherlock Holmes authority. Unlike many bibliophiles, he does not hesitate to come out into the open and collect books for the sake of the financial profit accruing therefrom. Mr. Starret makes a point of emphasizing the possibilities of this phase of book buying.

Most bookmen who succeed in having their scribblings published rather shun the question of profit and loss and take, on the whole, an altruistic view of the question of finance wherein the purchase and sale of rare or second-hand books are involved. After all, however, a bookman must live, if only to become the owner of more books, and if he can buy and sell at a profit, why keep his light hidden? Even the most avid and wealthy collector must, at some time or other, consider, at least briefly, the question as to whether or not he has bought judiciously, from the standpoint of price. One can hardly feel sorry if the books on his shelves are increasing in value rather than decreasing, and how is he to be justified unless some writer like Mr. Starret paves the way and gives him the benefit of his personal experiences? That is exactly what PENNY WISE AND BOOK FOOLISH purports to do.

Stevens, Henry (1819-1886)

> WHO SPOILS OUR NEW ENGLISH BOOKS ASKED AND ANSWERED BY HENRY STEVENS OF VERMONT. Woodcut illustrations and vignettes, 24mo, cloth. First edition, London, 1884.
>
> $3.50

Henry Stevens, an American engaged in bookselling in London, was the lifelong friend, book scout and agent of Mr. James Lenox, whose bequests of books and funds resulted in the founding of the New York Public Library. Stevens was also a veteran bibliographer and lover of books.

This particular little volume is a plea for better bookmaking and is dedicated "To The Memory of Two Old Friends, Charles Whittinghaus and William Pickering, Printer and Publisher, whose Beautiful Books are their Epitaphs."

Stevens, Henry (1819-1886)

> RECOLLECTIONS OF MR. JAMES LENOX OF NEW YORK AND THE FORMATION OF HIS LIBRARY. Two portraits, 12mo, cloth. London, 1886.
>
> $7.50

Stevens' principal clients were James Lenox and John Carter Brown, the founder of the John Carter Brown Library of Americana at Providence, Rhode Island.

This essay tells the story of how Mr. Lenox secured the many valuable and rare books which became the famous Lenox Collection. His library, willed to the people of New York, provided the foundation around which was created the public library of that city.

Thompson, James Westfall (1869-   )

BY-WAYS IN BOOKLAND. Small 8vo, blue cloth, gilt title. The Book Arts Club, Berkeley, 1935.

$2.50

Comprising a series of essays that are appealing both to the general reader and the book collector, Mr. Thompson in his book discusses the importance of libraries, describes the thrill of book hunting, and writes a charming history of Napoleon as a book lover. This volume is neither a textbook nor a tool for collectors but may well be used as collateral reading to increase one's general knowledge and to provide a diversion from the more serious aspects of collecting.

Tredwell, Daniel M. (1862-   )

A MONOGRAPH OF PRIVATELY ILLUSTRATED BOOKS: a Plea for Bibliomania. Royal 8vo, large paper, wrappers. Printed on handmade paper by De Vinne. Limited to 250 copies. Brooklyn, 1892.

$15.00

The same. Large 8vo, green buckram, calf label gilt. Brooklyn, 1892.

$5.00

The same. 8vo, vellum wrapper, decorative title and head of Rembrandt in red. Privately printed by the author. First edition, Brooklyn, 1891.

$10.00

Once the library of a bibliophile was not thought complete without examples of the art of grangerizing or privately illustrated books. Many books were robbed of their prints to supply the thousands of illustrations that were necessary at one time to satisfy the demand for volumes of this nature. While many such books are most complete in their pictorial description of the textual content, yet the practice of extra illustrating was carried to the point of absurdity when a simple volume might be extended to forty through the inlaying of plates torn from other and perhaps far more valuable books.

This work of Tredwell's describes the making, binding and cost of such books with examples as contained in the principal libraries in New York, Boston, Chicago and other cities. The book is supplemented by the inclusion of many interesting and curious facts relating to books in general. It is a useful addition to any collector's library and may be considered a standard work on the subject. It was originally prepared by the author as a paper to be read before the Rembrandt Club of Brooklyn, New York. Read in December 1880, it was privately printed in 1881 after extended additions to the text. The monograph was reprinted the following year, and in 1892 the large volume printed by Theodore L. De Vinne was brought out.

Tuer, Andrew White (1838-1900)

HISTORY OF THE HORN-BOOK. Large 8vo, full vellum, decorative title page in color, frontispiece, profusely illustrated, with 7 pockets containing imitation horn-books, 2 vols. London, 1896.

$35.00

This is a fascinating history of the very first reading materials that were used by children. Horn-books were described in an English dictionary printed in 1758 as "a leaf of written or printed paper pasted on a board, and covered with horn, for children to learn their letters by, and to prevent their being torn and daubed." Dr. Samuel Johnson called them "the first book of children, covered with horn to keep it unsoiled." In Dr. Brewer's DICTIONARY OF PHRASE AND FABLE, the horn-book is described as an alphabet book or board of oak about nine inches long and five or six wide, on which was printed the alphabet, the nine digits, and sometimes the Lord's Prayer. "It had," the Doctor says, "a handle and was covered in front with a sheet of thin horn to prevent it being soiled, and the back board was ornamented with a rude sketch of St. George and the Dragon. The board and its horn cover were held together by a narrow frame or border of brass."

Updike, Daniel Berkeley (1860   )

PRINTING TYPES, THEIR HISTORY, FORMS AND USES. A Study in Survivals. Illustrated, 2 vols., gilt top, boxed, 8vo. First edition, Merrymount Press, Cambridge, Massachusetts, 1922.

$30.00

BOOKS ABOUT BOOKS

This work by the head of the Merrymount Press, which he founded in 1893, is not likely to be superseded as a standard authority on typography for some little time. Issued in August, 1922, it was reprinted in 1923 and again in 1927. The first edition early attracted the attention of collectors to the extent that it now commands twice its published price of fifteen dollars.

The book is based upon lectures delivered by the author in a course on the technique of printing at the Harvard Graduate School of Business Administration from 1911-1916. As a result of his wide practical experience and scholarly research, Updike was eminently fitted to teach a course of this nature. Each year he added to his class room material, until his notes and data constituted a most complete study of the evolution and history of type designs. It is fortunate for the student of printing as well as for the book collector who can well afford some knowledge of the history of typography, that Updike decided to publish these lectures.

The book itself, as one might expect, is beautifully designed and printed. In addition, it is written in such an attractive style that the reader experiences little difficulty in becoming acquainted with the history of type and printing.

Updike, Daniel Berkeley (1860-   )

IN THE DAY'S WORK. 8vo., boards, buckram back. Cambridge, Mass., 1924.

$3.00

It is essential that the present day collector become acquainted with the aims and ideals of the master printers of his own time as well as with the ancient craftsmen of earlier days.

Updike is recommended, therefore, particularly to the younger readers of this volume, within whose lifetime, it is possible, may be witnessed a change in the social order that will discourage the pride in personal achievement which led a printer of Updike's character, and those others whose names are mentioned in his book, to strive constantly that he might produce, not only for his customers but primarily for his own satisfaction, the very best work that his shop could turn out.

Always a good craftsman and with the example of the great printers of all time before him, Updike in his book lays down his principles of work. It becomes a proper and fitting shelf companion to his PRINTING TYPES and contains much to delight and instruct the novice who is interested in printing and its allied problems.

While a noted scholar and idealist, Updike has been endowed as well with a large measure of practical business ability which has enabled him to become a practical printer without sacrificing any of his good taste. Associating since youth with publishing houses and never without the smell of ink in his nostrils, Updike founded, some forty-five years ago, the Merrymount Press, the imprint of which is now world famous.

Uzanne, Octave (1852-   )

THE BOOK-HUNTER IN PARIS, Studies among the bookstalls and the quays, Preface by Augustine Birrell. Royal 8vo, illustrations, cloth, t.e.g., uncut. Chicago, 1893.
$12.50

While it is said that the bookstalls of Paris no longer offer a "happy hunting ground" for the collector, yet they still exist and provide, even for the casual tourist, one of the most interesting and characteristic features of the city. Uzanne's enthusiasm for his subject, concerning which he has collected a great deal of fascinating information, is easily communicable to the reader. For the bookman about to visit Paris or for one who would know the history of the booksellers who maintain their picturesque stalls along the banks of the Seine, THE BOOK-HUNTER IN PARIS will provide the necessary data for an historical background of the sale of books in the first city of France.

An account is given of researches regarding second-hand booksellers of the past, of book hunters and book lovers and of famous libraries. Altogether it is a delightful volume for the modern collector who desires an entertaining and accurate picture of a book world and collectors no longer existent.

Van Hoesen, Henry B. (1885-   ) and Walter, Frank K. (1874-   )

BIBLIOGRAPHY ENUMERATIVE AND HISTORICAL, An Introductory Manual. 8vo, cloth. New York, 1928.
$7.50

This is indeed a book for the experienced collector as well as for the student. The authors were well equipped for their work, Van Hoesen being Librarian of Brown University and Walter Librarian of the University of Wisconsin. A vast store of working information is contained within its 519 pages. In effect, it is a dictionary of bibliography, as well as a text book. The author's only too brief account of some of the labor involved in the compilation and writing of the work, in connection with which over 30,000 subject and author index cards were prepared, may serve to indicate the thoroughness with which the subject is approached.

As a reference work in bibliography, this volume is probably unexcelled. In fact, the writer knows of no other publication that even approaches it in completeness. There is more concentrated information and data within its covers than may meet the eye at first glance. The result of the collaboration between Van Hoesen and Walter is not only a valuable source book from a technical point of view, but a volume that any collector can pick up and, by turning to a random page or section, find at once some data of interest and value to the pursuit of his hobby.

As the book has a list of 1500 separate bibliographies, the most important bibliographical works published may, with the aid of the index, be easily found.

Waldman, Milton (1895-   )

AMERICANA, The Literature of American History. 8vo. First Edition, New York, 1925.

$5.00

Invaluable as a standard reference work, this volume of Waldman's is essentially a history of histories. The collector of Americana will find this a most necessary and helpful book. The author has provided a concise, chronological account of the major books relating to the history of the discovery of America, its conquest and colonization.

Wegelin, Oscar (1876-   )

EARLY AMERICAN FICTION, 1744-1830, A compilation of the Titles of Works of Fiction, by Writers born or residing in North America, North of the Mexican Border and Printed previous to 1831. Third edition, corrected and enlarged, royal 8vo, cloth. New York, 1929.

$5.00

THE BIO-BIBLIOGRAPHY

Originally published by the author in 1902 from Stamford Connecticut, in an edition limited to 150 copies and reprinted in a limited edition in 1913, this work is the only bibliography devoted to early American fiction. Like its companion volume, EARLY AMERICAN POETRY, it is purely a subject bibliography.

It is included in this Bio-Bibliography, because the early fiction of any country, as represented by the efforts of its pioneer writers, reflects to a large extent the thoughts and modes of their day. The collector in search of a period or subject upon which to devote his time and funds might well attempt the acquisition of the titles described by Wegelin.

Williams, Iola A. (1890-   )

SEVEN EIGHTEENTH CENTURY BIBLIOGRAPHIES. 8vo, cloth. First edition, London, 1924.

$3.50

This volume is indicative of the author's capacity for research and his knowledge of the literature of the eighteenth century. It is included in this Bio-Bibliography not as an aid to all book collectors but simply to record a source of information for those interested in the following writers: John Galsworthy, William Shenstone, Mark Akenside, William Collins, Oliver Goldsmith, Charles Churchill, and Richard Brinsley Butler Sheridan.

Mr. Williams is an accurate bibliographer and a sincere bookman. In the essays with which he has prefaced five of the seven bibliographies included in his book, he has made an attempt to attract new readers to the authors whose works he describes.

Williams, Iola A. (1890-   )

THE ELEMENTS OF BOOK-COLLECTING. 8vo. First edition, London, 1927.

$3.00

Mr. Williams, who is well known in England as the bibliographical authority of the LONDON MERCURY, has capably employed his skill in preparing a book principally for the collector whose means and experience are limited. This book includes, as well, a great deal of practical information and suggestions which will prove of value to even the most experienced collector.

It is as a guide to the new collector, however, that Mr. Williams is to be particularly recommended. For instance, he tells his readers never to buy an imperfect book. Here is a first principle, a fundamental point, which far too many collectors, in their eagerness to buy, completely disregard.

The practice of book collecting does not consist simply in acquiring books, but is a highly developed art about which there is continually a great deal to learn. Not only does each new year bring a fresh crop of writers, whose books have possibilities of developing a demand among collectors, but new points in connection with recognized first editions are constantly being discovered. The successful collector must not only be careful of his original purchases, but must keep abreast of an ever increasing fund of information relative to the individual items on his library shelves.

Mr. Williams is an advocate of collecting by subject, and in this he has the support of the writer. While it seems probable that certain authors will always be collected and that a steady demand will continue for their books, yet concentrating on a single author is too much like having one's eggs all in the same basket. The writer believes that a greater contribution is made to existing literature and knowledge in collecting according to subject. Many more authors and a larger diversification can, of course, be obtained and a further addition to existing bibliographical knowledge can be made which will outweigh in real value the bibliographical points in favor of collecting the works of any individual author. These, after all, are frequently mere matters of opinion and of no great importance aside, perhaps, from a dollar and cents value.

Any supplement to a subject bibliography which a collector may make during his lifetime will be of importance to future students and add much to the sum total of existing knowledge.

Willis, James F. (1855-   )

BIBLIOPHILY or Booklove. Small 8vo, boards, cloth back, paper label, 83 pages. Cambridge, Massachusetts, 1921.

$1.00

The delightful essays contained in this slim little volume will appeal to the book lover and collector and provide a half-hour of entertaining reading. The collecting, reading and making of books as well as the love that men have for them, is discussed in six short, yet effective, chapters. While this item can usually be picked up in the second-hand shops for fifty cents, it is well worth its published price of one dollar and is, therefore, catalogued at this latter figure. The writer once bought three separate copies, attracted as much by their decorative paper cover and title page as by their contents. This may, possibly, be an example of book love as defined by Willis—"to perceive whatever is true and beautiful in books."

Willis also gives collectors one more excuse for their hobby, for he states that books "are not a luxury, but an essential of life; what food is to the body, books are to the soul and it is impossible to over-rate them." Surely no writer of books about books, not even Dibdin, has spoken more enthusiastically!

Winterich, John T. (1891-   )

A PRIMER OF BOOK COLLECTING. 12mo, cloth. First edition, New York, 1927.

$3.00

Thanks, presumably, to his early newspaper training and to his later experiences as one of the editors of *The Stars and Stripes*, the newspaper of the American Expeditionary Forces, and to his post as editor of *The American Legion Weekly*, plus an earnest cultivation of literary interests through personal contact with books and bookmen, Mr. Winterich has become one of the most interesting as well as practical of the modern writers of books about books. This particular item, so far as is known, is his first book on the subject of book-collecting. It was followed by COLLECTOR'S CHOICE and again a year later by BOOKS AND THE MAN. Mr. Winterich also turns out for the PUBLISHER'S WEEKLY a column of comments and notes on current happenings in the collector's world. In addition, he is a contributing editor to the COLOPHON which has published a number of his articles and writes a bi-monthly column for the SATURDAY REVIEW OF LITERATURE. As a prolific writer, the critics are having a hard time to keep up with his output. Unlike some present day writers on similar topics, Winterich has no axe to grind and is earnest in his endeavors to guide the collecting instinct of the beginning collector, yet he is sufficiently entertaining to hold the general reader's interest as well.

Briefly, the purpose of the author of A PRIMER OF BOOK COLLECTING is to instruct in the fundamentals of book collecting and to answer the questions which are bound to arise sooner or later in the mind of the collector. The word

BOOKS ABOUT BOOKS

"primer" is a good descriptive title, for this book is indeed as near an introductory text book on book collecting as has yet appeared. Incidentally, the success of this book must have been very gratifying to both publisher and author, for as the late George H. Sargent pointed out in his own review, Greenberg had not heretofore been noted as a publisher of bibliographical works and Winterich was a name which did not at that time appear in AMERICAN BOOK COLLECTORS.

Winterich has drawn largely upon his own experiences for copy and the opinions he expresses are his own. In discussing the cash value of books to the collector, however, he is forced to fall back upon the oft reiterated caution, namely, "books are a frozen investment," and "there are so many less wieldly things to gamble with and will be while Wall Street endures and fifty-two cards constitute a deck."

Winterich, John T. (1891-)

> COLLECTOR'S CHOICE. 8vo. First edition, New York, 1928.
>
> $3.00

Not content with writing and seeing successfully sold his first book on collecting, Mr. Winterich repeats his success with COLLECTOR'S CHOICE. In this second volume there is evidence of the author's increasing bibliographical knowledge. He is able to express himself conclusively on points of descriptive bibliography in connection with various individual authors. In his first book, Mr. Winterich kept close to the fundamental principles of book collecting which, of course, every earnest collector must master before he is competent to differentiate between a first edition and one which to all outward appearances purports to be the same thing.

In COLLECTOR'S CHOICE, issues, points and other variants are mentioned with confidence, although of necessity, for actual examples, the reader must refer to the individual bibliographies by other authors to which Mr. Winterich wisely calls attention. These first two books by Winterich have evolved in a natural order. The general background which the beginning collector can secure from a perusal of A PRIMER OF BOOK COLLECTING will permit of a greater understanding and appreciation of COLLECTOR'S CHOICE.

One outstanding feature of this book is the "bibliocathechism" in which Mr. Winterich presents his readers with a series of questions—one thousand in all. The answers are given in a different part of the book to satisfy one's curiosity after trying and failing. Mr. George H. Sargent once wrote that he secured a score of 625 and was thereupon heartily disgusted. The average collector would probably not come within fifteen per cent of Mr. Sargent's score. These questions are heartily recommended as sound mental exercise, and if the answers that one lacks are carefully looked up, much useful information and good bibliographical knowledge will be secured.

Winterich, John T. (1891-   )

> BOOKS AND THE MAN, with numerous full-page facsimile reproductions, half-tones, etc. 8vo, black cloth, t.e.g. First edition, New York, 1929.
>
> $5.00
>
> Limited edition, 210 copies
>
> $10.00

Again, Mr. Winterich scores with a third volume for book-collectors in this story of twenty famous books described in the biographical terms of the men who wrote them.

This book is a delightful source of information for the collector. Winterich not only writes entertainingly but instructively. None of his books are of a technical nature but have apparently been written with the general reader in mind as well as the avid collector. He easily ranks next to A. Edward Newton among modern writers on the subject of book collecting and deserves considerable credit for the industry represented by his books, particularly when it is considered that he is much younger than Newton and has not the advantages of a large fund of personal experiences to draw upon. He shows, however, an uncanny flair for research and bibliographical detail in his discussion of twenty "high point" authors and the origin of their most noted books. All of his writings are distinct contributions to literature for the collector, and Winterich is one of the most promising of present day writers on bibliographical subjects.

No one who reads Mr. Winterich's books can doubt his sincerity and love of books and collecting. In the past few years, there have been so many books "manufactured" on book collecting and allied subjects that it is refreshing to find one who writes with modest restraint on a topic that is so close to his heart. It is exceedingly doubtful that one could remain immune from the disease bibliomania after an evening in company with Winterich's books.

Winterich, John T. (1891-   )

> EARLY AMERICAN BOOKS AND PRINTING. 8vo., red buckram, t.e.g., illustrated, uncut, large paper, boxed. Limited to 300 signed copies. Boston and New York, 1935.
> $10.00

Beginning with the earliest Americana, Winterich has produced a book for students of bibliography and collectors, specializing in items included in the broad field covered by its title. While the text of the volume goes back to the letters of Columbus, most readers will be interested in the section devoted to Colonial American authors, printing and publishers. Some interesting stories are told of the earliest American books and libraries and the factual material has been brought up to the time of the Early American authors. The book has a useful index and is beautifully printed.

Wise, Thomas James (1859-1937)

> THE ASHLEY LIBRARY, A Catalogue of Printed Books, Manuscripts, and Autograph Letters, profusely illustrated. 10 Vols., 4to, buckram, t.e.g., uncut, limited to 200 copies. Privately printed, London, 1922-1930.
> $400.00

Aside from its book descriptions and invaluable contributions to bibliographical sources of English literature during the past three hundred years, the most astonishing feature of the ASHLEY LIBRARY CATALOGUE is that Mr. Wise not only collected every book he describes, without the assistance of agents, but he also wrote every word of the manuscript for the printer in his own hand.

This is one of the great library catalogues. It contains valuable collections of Nash, Bew, Johnson, Shirley, Milton, Wordsworth, Shelley, Coleridge, Keats, Swinburne, Conrad and others. As the introduction states, "There is scarcely a single poet or dramatist of repute whose name cannot be found here; this catalogue is superior, not so much for the books it describes but the way in which it describes them."

The ASHLEY LITERARY CATALOGUE is as much a history of English literature as any text book ever written and it is far more fascinating. It is, though, a work for the expert rather than for the average collector, and it is to be regretted that

THE BIO-BIBLIOGRAPHY

Mr. Ashley did not include more of personal reminiscence in order that the volumes might have a greater interest and value to the younger collector.

Volume six with an introduction by Mr. A. Edward Newton is the only one of the ten sponsored by an American author. This makes the CATALOGUE a Newton item, although, with due respect to A.E.N., it is because of its own representative value rather than its association interest that it is here reviewed!

Thomas James Wise spent over forty years collecting and writing about books. In particular, he wrote about his own special libraries. In his bibliographical work he has endeared himself to booklovers and performed a lasting service in making available the results of his studies and collecting activities. Dying in 1937 at seventy-seven years of age, Dr. Wise was one of England's greatest bibliographical authorities.

When the first volume of the ASHLEY LIBRARY CATALOGUE was issued in 1922, it was announced by some booksellers that it would undoubtedly be completed in three volumes. However, such an extensive contribution to bibliography could not be condensed and the final result embraced ten volumes enumerating some ten thousand books.

As an exacting and discriminating collector since boyhood days and with the means to gratify to the fullest extent the grandest passion in which a man can indulge, Ashley amassed one of the most famous private libraries in England. Its catalogue will continue to occupy a high and permanent place in English bibliographical literature.

CHAPTER III

Magazine References

As the literature of book collecting is relatively slight, any addition that will give the collector some further reference material may not be out of place. It is, therefore, with this thought in mind that the following brief bibliography of magazine articles relative to Book Collecting, Books about Books, Bibliography, Book Selling, Rare Books, Libraries, Manuscripts, and First Editions as published from January 1, 1900 to June 10, 1937 has been compiled. It is probably far from complete, but may serve as a foundation for later contributions. It is interesting to note the extent and character of such articles that have been written, mainly for popular consumption, over the past thirty-seven years.

1900

Birrell, A.	HOW TO KNOW A GOOD BOOK. *Current Literature*, May
Borton, F. S.	BOOK-HUNTER IN MEXICO. *Bookman*, February
Warner, G. F.	ILLUMINATED MANUSCRIPTS IN THE BRITISH MUSEUM. *Athenaeum*, March 24.
Anonymous	GREATEST BOOKS OF THE CENTURY. *Outlook*, December 1.
Anonymous	AUGUSTIN DALY LIBRARY. *Athenaeum*, March 24.
Anonymous	HISTORICAL MANUSCRIPTS. American Historical Association *Report*

1901

Bishop, W. W.	BOOK-HUNTING IN ROME. *Bookman*, February
Curtis, G. P.	SOME LOST MANUSCRIPT TREASURES. *Catholic World*, July
Hodder, F. H.	EARLY ANTI-SLAVERY PUBLICATIONS. *Dial*, November 1.
Livingston, L. S.	ARNOLD SALES. *Bookman*, March
Macy, C.	UNIQUE COLLECTION. *Outlook*, February 2.
North, E. D.	NOTES OF RARE BOOKS. *Book Buyer*, June
North, E. D.	THOMAS BAILEY ALDRICH; ORIGINAL EDITIONS OF HIS WORKS. *Book Buyer*, May

MAGAZINE REFERENCES

O'Hagan, A.	WORLD'S RAREST BOOKS. *Munsey*, May.
Pennell, E. R.	MY COOKERY BOOKS. *Atlantic Monthly*, June
Roberts, W.	BOOK COLLECTING AS AN INVESTMENT. *Fortnightly*, September
Warner, G. F.	ILLUMINATED MANUSCRIPTS IN THE BRITISH MUSEUM. *Athenaeum*, September 14.
Anonymous	COLLECTION OF T. J. MCKEE. *Critic*, March
Anonymous	COLLECTION OF W. H. ARNOLD. *Critic*, March
Anonymous	NOTES OF A BOOK COLLECTOR. *Critic*, October
Anonymous	BOOKS ABOUT BOOKS. *Outlook*, October 26.
Anonymous	GREATEST BOOKS OF THE CENTURY. *Dial*, January 1.
Anonymous	BLACK BOOKS OF LINCOLN'S INN. *Current Literature*, July
Anonymous	MANUSCRIPTS IN THE NEW YORK PUBLIC LIBRARY. *Nation*, August 8.
Anonymous	MANUSCRIPTS OF THE CONDE MUSEUM. *Nation*, February 7, 21.
Anonymous	RAWLINSON MANUSCRIPTS CATALOGUED. *Nation*, March 28.

1902

Black, A.	COURT BIBLE. *Atlantic Monthly*, December
Braunling, G. A.	OLDEST ENGLISH PRINTED BOOK. *Era*, August
Fletcher, W. Y.	ENGLISH BOOK COLLECTORS. *Athenaeum*, May 17.
Hadden, J. C.	FOUR THOUSAND POUND BIBLE AND OTHERS. *Living Age*, July 19.
Hoare, H. W.	LINEAGE OF THE ENGLISH BIBLE. *Harpers*, March
Kenyon, F. G.	LINEAGE OF THE CLASSICS. *Harpers*, August
Lang, A.	BIBLIOMANIA. *Living Age*, August 16.
Lincoln, C. H.	MANUSCRIPTS IN THE LIBRARY. *Athenaeum*, May 17.
Mather, Frank J.	BOOK COLLECTORS AND OTHERS. *Nation*, January 30.
North, E. D.	NOTES OF RARE BOOKS. *Book Buyer*, June, October
Pennell, E. R.	MY COOKERY BOOKS. *Atlantic Monthly*, August, November
Roberts, W.	FOUNTAINE LIBRARY. *Athenaeum*, May 17.
Roberts, W.	HENRY WHITE LIBRARY. *Athenaeum*, April 5.
Roberts, W.	VOYNICH EXHIBITION OF UNKNOWN BOOKS. *Athenaeum*, June 14.

BOOKS ABOUT BOOKS

Anonymous	RICH PEOPLE AND THE OLD-BOOK MARKET. *Nation*, May 1.
Anonymous	STRAWBERRY HILL PRESS. *Athenaeum*, April 12.
Anonymous	CURIOSITIES OF BOOK-SALES. *Book Buyer*, March
Anonymous	HIBBERT SALE. *Athenaeum*, April 19.

1903

Andrews, W. L.	VAGARIES OF BOOK-COLLECTORS. *Lamp*, March.
Bocock, J. P.	LITTLE STORIES IN RARE BOOKS. *Harper's Weekly*, January 31.
Harrison, A.	BIBLES OLD AND NEW. *Munsey*, May
Herrick, C. T.	CULT OF THE BIBLIOPHILE. *Era*, August
Hobson, J. P.	UPS AND DOWNS OF OLD BOOKS. *Living Age*, March 7.
Hodgkin, J. E.	RARIORA. *Athenaeum*, January 3.
Mather, Frank J.	EDITIONS DE LUXE. *Nation*, November 26.
Anonymous	OLDEST BOOK IN THE WORLD. *Scientific American*, June 13.
Anonymous	AGE OF A BOOK. *Harper's Weekly*, October 17.
Anonymous	ILLUMINATED MANUSCRIPTS AT SOUTH KENSINGTON. *Modern Art*, July

1904

Brady, C. T.	UNIQUE LIBRARY. *Critic*, September
Collingwood, W. G.	RUSKIN'S BIBLES. *Living Age*, February
Williams, H. S.	PRIMITIVE BOOK. *Harper's Weekly*, May

1905

Benson, A. C.	BOOKS. *Living Age*, August 26.
Benson, A. C.	BOOKS. *College Window*, August 26.
Conrad, J.	BOOKS. *Living Age*, August 19.
Holland, C.	ROMANCE OF OLD-BOOK COLLECTING. *Living Age*, January 28.
Lamont, Hammond	ROWFANT BOOK. *Nation*, April 6.
Lane, W. C.	BIBLIOGRAPHY IN AMERICA. *Dial*, February 1.
Lang, A.	BOOKMEN'S BOOKS. *Living Age*, November 25.
Laugel, Auguste	EARLY PRINTED BOOKS IN THE CHANTILLY LIBRARY. *Nation*, May 11.
Scott, M. A.	BOOK FROM THE LIBRARY OF THE EARL OF LEICESTER. February 11.

MAGAZINE REFERENCES

Woodward, B. B.	BIBLIOGRAPHICAL DEFINITIONS. *Athenaeum*, February 11.

1906

Adler, E. N.	ABOUT HEBREW MANUSCRIPTS. *Nation*, January 4.
Bloomfield, M.	LONG LOST MANI BIBLE. *Harper's Monthly Magazine*, March
Drew, M.	GLADSTONE'S LIBRARY AT ST. DEINIOL'S HAWARDEN. *Nineteenth Century*, June
Hulme, W. H.	VALUABLE MIDDLE ENGLISH MANUSCRIPT. *Modern Philology*, July
Livingston, Arthur	MOST VALUABLE AMERICAN PRINTED BOOK. *Nation*, July 5.
Wright, J.	HISTORIC BIBLES IN AMERICA. *Nation*, October 11.
Anonymous	MORGAN MANUSCRIPTS. *Nation*, October 18.
Anonymous	PERKIN LIBRARY. *Science*, October 26.
Anonymous	AUCTION PRICES OF BOOKS. *Outlook*, August 4.

1907

Boyd, J. S.	SECOND HAND BOOKS. *New England Magazine*, March
Evans, C.	AMERICAN BIBLIOGRAPHY. *Nation*, October 31.
Lamont, Hammond	PROFESSION OF BOOK-AGENT. *Nation*, February 14.
Wallace, W. S.	AMONG RELICS OF THE PAST. *Canadian Magazine*
Anonymous	FIRST EDITIONS OF AMERICAN AUTHORS. *Nation*, September
Anonymous	FOUR CENTURIES OF BOOK PRICES. *Review of Reviews*, April

1908

Clark, C. U.	PHOTOGRAPHIC REPRODUCTIONS OF MANUSCRIPTS. *Nation*, March 19.
Drew, M.	GLADSTONE'S LIBRARY AT ST. DEINIOL'S HAWARDEN. *Living Age*, August 18.
Muscus	MEDIAEVAL BOOKS AND BOOK PRICES. *Contemporary Review*, August
Anonymous	BERNARD QUARITCH AND OTHERS. *Living Age*, January 18.

1909

Bruce, H. A.	TREASURE ROOM IN HARVARD UNIVERSITY LIBRARY. *Outlook*, November 27.
Livingston, Arthur	HOE'S PRIVATE LIBRARY. *Nation*, September 30.

BOOKS ABOUT BOOKS

Livingston, Arthur	J. CHESTER CHAMBERLAIN COLLECTION OF FIRST EDITIONS OF AMERICAN AUTHORS. *Nation*, February 25.

1910

Bigelow, M. O.	BOOKS. *Independent*, March 10.
Forman, H. B.	PLEASURES OF A BOOK-MAN. *Atlantic Monthly*, June
Ford, W. C.	USE OF MANUSCRIPTS. *Nation*, July 21.
Galt, H. R.	LIBRARY OF AUTOGRAPHED BOOKS. *World's Work*, April
Hoffman, M. D.	MOST BEAUTIFUL BOOK IN THE WORLD. *Scribner's Magazine*, October
Konkle, B. A.	INK AND MANUSCRIPTS. *Nation*, August 11.
Livingston, Arthur	LIBRARY OF HENRY HUTH. *Nation*, November 2.
Livingston, Arthur	LIBRARY OF HOE. *Nation*, May 4.
Livingston, Arthur	HOE'S COLLECTION OF ENGLISH LITERATURE OF THE SIXTEENTH AND SEVENTEENTH CENTURIES. *Nation*, April 20.
Lucy, H.	SOME OF A HUNDRED BEST BOOKS. *Living Age*, July 23.

1911

Morin, V.	OUR PRINTED TREASURES. *Canadian Magazine*, June
Anonymous	EXHIBITION AT THE BRITISH MUSEUM OF BIBLES AND DOCUMENTS. *Nation*, March 30.
Anonymous	LOVE OF BOOKS. *Living Age*, November 25.
Anonymous	GREAT SALE OF RARE BOOKS; HOE COLLECTION. *Outlook*, May 13.

1912

Blathwayt, R.	ROMANCE OF THE SALE ROOM. *Fortnightly Review*, November
Burgess, G.	BATTLE OF THE BOOKS, FOUGHT BY COLLECTORS OVER THE RARE VOLUMES OF THE HOE LIBRARY. *Collier's*, February 10.
Collins, F. A.	LITERARY TREASURES OF THE HUMBLE. *Bookman*, June
Currier, C. W.	DISCOVERY OF HISTORIC MANUSCRIPTS OF MEXICO. *Bulletin* Pan American Union, September
Jackson, J.	SPORT OF MONEY KINGS. *World's Work*, November
Johnston, W. D.	SPECIAL COLLECTIONS IN LIBRARIES IN THE UNITED STATES. United States Bureau of Education *Bulletin*

MAGAZINE REFERENCES

L. S. L.	HUTH LIBRARY. *Nation*, August 1.
L. S. L.	LIBRARY FORMED BY BEVERLY CHEW. *Nation*, October 31.
Livingston, Arthur	THIRD PART OF THE ROBERT HOE LIBRARY. *Nation*, April 4.
Livingston, Arthur	LIBRARY OF WILLIAM W. ALLIS. *Nation*, March 14.
Roberts, W.	RECENT BOOK SALES. *Nineteenth Century and After*, November
Anonymous	BOOKS OF TODAY AND FIFTY YEARS AGO. *Literary Digest*, February 17.
Anonymous	CLASSICAL RUBBISH. *Dial*, October 1.
Anonymous	ANCIENT MANUSCRIPTS. *American Homes*, May
Anonymous	PIERPONT MORGAN'S LIBRARIAN. *Literary Digest*, May 4.
Anonymous	LOSS OF A YOUNG BOOK LOVER. *Literary Digest*, June 15.
Anonymous	NEW BIBLE MANUSCRIPT. *Living Age*, May 25.

1913

Cockerell, T. D. A.	DATING OF BOOKS. *Dial*, July 1.
Hervey, J. L.	TRIBULATIONS OF AN AMATEUR BOOK BUYER. *Atlantic Monthly*, September
Jackson, A. V. W.	PERSIAN MANUSCRIPTS. *Nation*, June 9.
King, F. A.	COMPLETE COLLECTOR. *Bookman*, January and February
Livingston, Arthur	THIRD PORTION, HUTH LIBRARY. *Nation*, May 22.
Livingston, Arthur	BERNARD QUARITCH. *Nation*, September 4.
Livingston, Arthur	EDWARD N. CRANE, COLLECTOR OF AMERICANA. *Nation*, February 20.
Livingston, Arthur	LIBRARY OF THE LATE MATTHEW C. D. BORDEN. *Nation*, January 23.
Livingston, Arthur	SALE OF SIR THOMAS PHILLIPS MANUSCRIPTS. *Nation*, May 1.
Morton, E. P.	SCOTT AND THE THREE-VOLUME NOVEL. *Nation*, April 3.
Strunsky, Simeon	RARE BOOKS. *Nation*, November 27.
Anonymous	HOW THE NEW BOOKS HAVE MORE THAN DOUBLED IN TWENTY-TWO YEARS. *Literary Digest*, March 1.
Anonymous	OLDEST BOOK IN THE WORLD. *Living Age*, December 20.
Anonymous	MORGAN BIBLES AND PRAYER BOOKS. *Literary Digest*

1914

Maclaren, I.	BOOKS AND BOOKMEN. *Books and Bookmen*.
Nevins, Allan	SCHOLAR, BOOK-COLLECTOR. *Nation*, December 31.

BOOKS ABOUT BOOKS

Portor, L. S.	BOOKS ABOUT BOOKS. *Woman's Home Companion*, March
Spectator	CLUB CONVERSATION ON READING AND BOOK-COLLECTING. *Outlook*, March 21.
Anonymous	FINDING LOST TREASURES. *American Homes*, May
Anonymous	BANISHED BOOKS. *Dial*, September 1.
Anonymous	MORE ENGLISH TREASURES FOR AMERICA. *Literary Digest*, April 4.

1915

Lee, J. T.	LUTHER S. LIVINGSTON: THE MAN AND HIS WORK. *Nation*, August 26 and September 2.
Newton, A. E.	AMENITIES OF BOOK-COLLECTING. *Atlantic Monthly*, March, April
Parry, E.	BURIED TREASURE. *Living Age*, June 19.

1916

Roosevelt, B. and K.	TWO BOOK-HUNTERS IN SOUTH AMERICA. *Bulletin Pan American Union*, December; *Bookman*, October
Anonymous	LAST WORD ON BOOKBUYING. *Literary Digest*, August 26.
Anonymous	BOOKWORMS SURVIVING WAR. *Literary Digest*, February 5.

1917

Brooks, C. S.	ON BUYING OLD BOOKS. *Yale Review*, October
de Montgomery, J. E. G.	BIBLIOPHILE MOVES ON. *Contemporary Review*, August; *Living Age*, November 3.
Anonymous	FUTURES IN RARE BOOKS. *Literary Digest*, September 22.
Anonymous	TRAILING BOOK SPENDTHRIFTS. *Literary Digest*, August 4.
Anonymous	BEST SELLERS OF A CENTURY AGO. *Independent*, April 14.

1918

Clark, M. V.	BOOKS BY THE YARD. *Nation*, April 4.
Dorr, C. H.	LURE OF OLD BOOKS. *Art World*, October
Dorr, C. H.	LITERARY TREASURES OF HERSCHEL V. JONES. *Art World*, November
Nevins, Allan	AMERICA'S WEALTH IN MANUSCRIPTS. *Nation*, January 31.
Sargent, G. H.	RARE BOOKS IN WARTIME. *Bookman*, November

MAGAZINE REFERENCES

Anonymous   WHERE OUR RARE BOOKS COME FROM. *Literary Digest*, February 16.

1919

Boas, F. S.   SELLING THE NATIONS HEIRLOOMS. *Nineteenth Century and After*, August

Clark, M. V.   BOOK ADDICT. *Bookman*, July

LeGallienne, R.   BOOKS I HAVE LOVED AND LOST. *Bookman*, October

Sargent, G. H.   COLLECTORS AND DEALERS. *Bookman*, October

Sargent, G. H.   SHOULD COLLECTORS READ BOOKS? *Bookman*, August

Sargent, G. H.   NEW FASHIONS IN RARE BOOKS. *Bookman*, April

Scapecchi, C.   ART OF MAKING BEAUTIFUL BOOKS. *Touchstone*, September

Scoggin, G. C.   AS TO BIBLIOMANIA. *Unpartizan Review*, October

Shackford, M. H.   FOR BETTER BIBLIOGRAPHIES. *Educational Review*, May

Williams, L.   AMONG THE OLD BOOK STALLS. *Review*, October 18.

Anonymous   WORLD'S COSTLIEST BOOK; THE FIRST COLLECTED EDITIONS OF SHAKESPEARE, DATED 1619; PREVIOUSLY OF THE MARSDEN J. PERRY SHAKESPEARE COLLECTION. *Literary Digest*, November 15.

Anonymous   HIGH PRICES FOR MANUSCRIPTS. *Literary Digest*, August 2.

1920

Arnold, W. H.   MAKING OF A BOOK-COLLECTOR. *Century*, July

Eaton, W. P.   REDUCING THE HIGH COST OF COLLECTING. *Bookman*, July

Gaillard, E. W.   BOOK LARCENY PROBLEM. *Library Journal*, March 15, April 1.

Lydenberg, H. M. and others   IMPORTATIONS FROM GERMANY. *Library Journal*, April 15.

McConn, M.   OF MAKING MANY BOOKS. *New Republic*, July 7.

Sargent, G. H.   PROBLEM OF THE PLUGS. *Bookman*, February

Sargent, G. H.   AUCTIONITIS. *Bookman*, September

Wells, G.   EVOLUTION OF THE BOOK-COLLECTOR. *Bookman*, April

Van Doren, Carl   BROKER IN BOOKS. *Nation*, March 20.

Anonymous   DAMNING BIBLIOPHILISM. *Literary Digest*, April 10.

Anonymous   MR. PUNCH'S REGRET OVER LOST LITERARY TREASURES. *Literary Digest*, October 30.

BOOKS ABOUT BOOKS

Anonymous	NAPOLEON OF BOOK BUYERS. *Outlook*, March 17.
Anonymous	WALL STREET METHODS WITH RARE BOOKS; ACTIVITIES OF G. D. SMITH. *Literary Digest*, February 21.
Anonymous	GUESSING THE DURABLE BOOKS. *Literary Digest*, September 18.
Anonymous	COLOPHONS OF AMERICAN PUBLISHERS. *Review*, January 17.

1921

Abernethy, J.	BOOK-LOVERS PROTEST. *Library Journal*, September 15.
Arnold, W. H.	BOOK HUNTER'S GARNER. *Century*, April
Bird, J. M.	ROGER BACON MANUSCRIPT. *Scientific American Monthly*, June
Birrell, A.	ROMANCE OF BOOK DISCOVERY. *Public Libraries*, February
Blumenthal, W. H.	WORLD'S MOST CURIOUS BOOKS. *Bookman*, March
Jordan, L. M.	ADVENTURES OF A BOOK-BUYER. *Public Libraries*, April
Porter, H. C.	AMENITIES OF BOOKSELLING. *Atlantic Monthly*, February
Anonymous	BOOK LOVERS OF TOMORROW. *Bookman*, February
Anonymous	ROGER BACON MANUSCRIPT, WHAT IT LOOKS LIKE AND A DISCUSSION OF THE PROBABILITIES OF DECIPHERMENT. *Scientific American Monthly*, May 28.
Anonymous	ROGER BACON'S CIPHER MANUSCRIPT. *Review of Reviews*, July
Anonymous	SECRET MANUSCRIPTS OF THE BRITISH MUSEUM. *Living Age*, October 8.

1922

Arnold, W. H.	BOOK HUNTER'S GARNER. *Century*, October
Cotton, A. L.	ASSOCIATION BOOKS. *Contemporary Review*, October
Duncan, Eleanor	FAVORITE BOOKS OF THE LIGHT FINGERED. *Library Journal*, October 15.
Haight, M. M.	RARE BOOK TREASURES FOR $1.25. *Mentor*, June
Holliday, R. C.	WITH THE COMPLIMENTS OF THE AUTHOR. *Bookman*, December
Anonymous	NONSENSE LIBRARY AND OTHER LIBRARIES. *Living Age*, December 16.

1923

Digby, B.	TALKING OF BOOKS. *Living Age*, June 23.

MAGAZINE REFERENCES

Jenison, M.	AND NOW IT MUST BE SOLD. *Bookman*, March
Morley, C.	RARE BOOKS. *Literary Review*, January 20.
Richardson, E. C.	BOOK-HUNTING IN GERMANY. *Public Libraries*, February
Walpole, H.	MR. POVERTY-STRUCK BOOK COLLECTOR. *Bookman*, October
Wells, H. G.	TEN MOST IMPORTANT BOOKS IN THE WORLD. *American Magazine*, April; *Current Opinion*, May

1924

Bennett, A.	BOOKS AND BOOK BUYING. *Woman's Home Companion*, February
Brooks, J. E.	BEAUTIFUL PRINTED BOOKS. *International Studio*, November
Chancellor, E. B.	COST OF BOOKS. *Fortnightly Review*, January
Chapman, J. J.	DANGER OF BOOKS. *Independent*, December 6.
Hopkins, F. M.	WORLD OF RARE BOOKS. *Saturday Review of Literature*, Weekly numbers beginning August 2.
Pearson, E. L.	SPORT OF KINGS. *Outlook*, February 13.
Sargent, G. H.	MODERN FIRST EDITIONS. *American Mercury*, February
Wells, G.	LURE OF COLLECTING. *Saturday Review of Literature*, January 17.
Anonymous	CHOOSING THE CENTURY'S BOOKS. *Current Opinion*, May
Anonymous	CASE FOR THE FIRST EDITION. *Bookman*, December

1925

Anderson, E. H.	BOOK THEFTS. *Library Journal*, March 15.
Benet, S. V.	LITERARY TREASURE. *Bookman*, December
Hanson, J. C. M.	NEWSPAPERS AND PERIODICALS; SOME BIBLIOGRAPHICAL AND BIBLIOTHECAL PROBLEMS. *Library Journal*, September 15.
Kaiser, J. B.	AROUND THE BIBLIOGRAPHICAL CORNER, SOME PROJECTED BIBLIOGRAPHIC AND REFERENCE COMPILATIONS. *Library Journal*, September 1.
Melcher, F. G.	BOOKSELLING. *Saturday Review of Literature*, April 11.
Potter, E. G.	LITERARY TREASURES OF MILLS COLLEGE. *Overland*, January
Starrett, V.	HAVE YOU A TAMARLANE IN YOUR ATTIC? *Saturday Evening Post*, June 27.

BOOKS ABOUT BOOKS

Starrett, V.	DIAMOND IN THE DUST HEAP. *Saturday Evening Post*, November 28.
Anonymous	MODERN FIRSTS. *Living Age*, March 7.
Anonymous	ON BEING COLLECTED. *Living Age*, January 24.
Anonymous	PEDIGREED BOOKS FOR MILLIONAIRES. *Literary Digest*, February 21.
Anonymous	MAKING OF THE LOEB CLASSICAL LIBRARY. *Living Age*, April 25.

1926

Abbott, L. F.	BOOK COLLECTING. *Outlook*, June 2.
Ainsworth, J.	AROUND PARIS WITH A BOOK WORM. *Travel*, July
Comstock, H.	BROOKLYN MUSEUM'S MANUSCRIPTS. *International Studio*, November
Dickson, S. B.	PATCHQUILT OF BIBLOPHILIA. *Overland*, August
Holliday, R. C.	SPREAD OF THE BOOK. *Bookman*, June
Hopkins, F. M.	WORLD OF RARE BOOKS. *Saturday Review of Literature*, Weekly numbers 1926-7
Morley, C.	UNWASHED CLAWSON COLLECTION OF TUDOR AND STUART BOOKS. *Saturday Review of Literature*, May 15.
Richardson, E. C.	IMMEDIATE CO-OPERATION FOR BIBLIOGRAPHICAL RESULTS. *Literary Journal*, February 15.
Starrett, V.	ON THE REBINDING OF BOOKS. *Saturday Evening Post*, November 13.
Starrett, V.	ABC OF FIRST EDITIONS. *Saturday Evening Post*, June 5.
Strohl, J.	SCOPE OF BIBLIOGRAPHIES. *Science*, February 26.
Wright, C. H.	SELECTION OF BOOKS. *Contemporary*, June
Anonymous	SOME STRANGE BOOK-COLLECTORS. *Nineteenth Century and After*, November
Anonymous	FIRST EDITIONS. *Living Age*, November 15.
Anonymous	MELK COPY OF THE GUTENBERG BIBLE. *International Studio*, June
Anonymous	RECORD PRICE FOR THE GUTENBERG BIBLE. *Literary Journal*, March
Anonymous	GUTENBERG BIBLE FETCHES $106,000. *Catholic World*, March

1927

Boyd, T.	BIBLIOPHILE. *Bookman*, January

MAGAZINE REFERENCES

Cannon, C. L.	PRICE OF BOOKS. *Outlook*, June 22.
Duncan, Eleanor	HENRY E. HUNTINGTON LIBRARY. *Library Journal*, June 1.
Hale, G. E.	HUNTINGTON LIBRARY AND ART GALLERY; THE NEW PLAN OF RESEARCH. *Scribner's*, July; *Review of Reviews*, July
Hopkins, F. M.	WORLD OF RARE BOOKS. *Saturday Review of Literature*, August 2, 1924 to October 15, 1927.
Jones, H. Bedford	ONE NIGHT AT CAHILL'S. *Bookman*, August
Leach, H. S.	SHORT TITLE CATALOGUE OF ENGLISH BOOKS BEFORE 1640. *Library Journal*, September 1.
Metthews, J. M.	MASTERPIECES. *Saturday Review of Literature*, January 1.
Newton, A. E.	WHAT TO COLLECT AND WHY. *Saturday Evening Post*, September 24.
Rollins, Carl P. & Winship, George P.	COMPLEAT COLLECTOR. *Saturday Review of Literature*, Weekly numbers from November 5.
Rosenbach, A. S. W.	TALKING OF OLD BOOKS (A. Strakosch, Editor). *Saturday Evening Post*, January 22.
Rosenbach, A. S. W.	MILLION DOLLAR BOOKSHELF (A. Strakosch, Editor). *Saturday Evening Post*, February 12.
Rosenbach, A. S. W.	AMONG OLD MANUSCRIPTS (A. Strakosch, Editor). *Saturday Evening Post*, March 5.
Rosenbach, A. S. W.	SOME LITERARY FORGERIES (A. Strakosch, Editor). *Saturday Evening Post*, March 19.
Rosenbach, A. S. W.	AND SOLD TO—: (A. Strakosch, Editor). *Saturday Evening Post*, April 23.
Rosenbach, A. S. W.	EARLY AMERICAN CHILDREN'S BOOKS (A. Strakosch, Editor). *Saturday Evening Post*, May 14.
Rosenbach, A. S. W.	OLD BIBLES (A. Strakosch, Editor). *Saturday Evening Post*, June 4.
Rosenbach, A. S. W.	COLLECTOR'S BEST BET (A. Strakosch, Editor). *Saturday Evening Post*, July 2.
Rosenbach, A. S. W	EARLIEST CHRISTMAS BOOKS. *Ladies Home Journal*, December
Walter, F. K.	NEED OF AN INTRODUCTORY MANUAL IN BIBLIOGRAPHY. *Library Journal*, August
Anonymous	WORTH A HUNDRED TIMES ITS WEIGHT IN GOLD; EARLY AMERICAN BOOK IN THE INDIAN TONGUE. *Mentor*, October
Anonymous	THE BIGGEST BOOK AND THE SMALLEST. *Mentor*, March

BOOKS ABOUT BOOKS

1928

Burgess, I. J.	ENGLISH ILLUMINATED MANUSCRIPTS. *International Studio*, May
Duncan, Eleanor	ON CUTTING UP RARE BOOKS. *Library Journal*, March 15.
Fisher, D. H.	MEDICI ACCOUNT BOOKS. *American Historical Review*, July
Haselden, R. B.	MANUSCRIPTS IN THE HUNTINGTON LIBRARY. *Library Journal*, September 15.
Newton, A. E.	THIS BOOK-COLLECTING GAME. *Review and Outlook*, November 21.
Rose, D.	DIME MUSEUM; BUYING GOOD BOOKS FOR TEN CENTS AT A SECOND-HAND BOOK STORE. *North American*, August
Salade, R. F.	MOST VALUABLE PRINTED BOOK IN THE WORLD; 42 LINE BIBLE. *Industrial Arts Magazine*, June
Scott, T.	LIBRARY OF GEORGIAN AND VICTORIAN LITERATURE; JEROME KERN'S COLLECTION OF FIRST EDITIONS. *International Studio*, December
Schreiber, W. L.	MIGRATION OF EUROPEAN COLLECTIONS TO AMERICA (Translated by H. M. Lydenberg). *Library Journal*, October 5.
Smith, P. J.	COLLECTOR'S TRIFLES. *Overland*, July
Valentine, U.	GUTENBERG AND HIS BOOK OF BOOKS. *International Studio*, September
Walter, F. K.	SAFEGUARDING RARE AND EXPENSIVE BOOKS IN UNIVERSITY AND REFERENCE LIBRARIES. *Library Journal*, September 15.
Anonymous	IF YOU KNOW WHAT I MEAN. *Independent*, April 21.
Anonymous	ALICE IN A FINANCIAL WONDERLAND. *Literary Digest*, April 21.
Anonymous	TACTLESS PERFORMANCE? ALICE IN WONDERLAND. *Literary Digest*, April 28.

1929

Benchely, R.	DO I HEAR TWENTY THOUSAND? SHELLEY, SWIFT, TENNYSON AND OTHERS DISCUSS THE JEROME KERN SALE. *Bookman*, March
Bennett, W.	REBUTTAL ON THE BROKEN TYPE THEORY; REJOINDER TO M. K. DUTTON. *Publishers' Weekly*, December 21.

MAGAZINE REFERENCES

Cochran, M. R.	ACQUISITION AND CARE OF SPECIAL COLLECTIONS. *Library Journal*, March 15.
Curle, R.	WHAT BOOKS TO COLLECT. *World's Work*, June
Day, A.	RARE BOOKS; HOW THE BULLS HAVE INVADED THE MARKET. *Century*, August
Eckel, J. C.	POINTS FOR BOOK-COLLECTORS. *World's Work*, July
Greer, M. R.	MISSING BOOKS. *Wilson Bulletin*, April
Hopkins, F. M.	OLD AND RARE BOOKS. *Publishers' Weekly*, Weekly numbers 1929 to 1932.
Hopkins, F. M.	AMERICAN FIRSTS. *Publishers' Weekly*, August 31.
Hopkins, F. M.	QUERIES AND REPLIES. *Publishers' Weekly*, Nov. 16.
Hopkins, F. M.	EARLY AMERICAN JUVENILES. *Publishers' Weekly*, November 16.
Jones, F. C.	SPOIL FROM THE ENGLISH MONASTIC LIBRARIES. *Contemporary Review*, July; *Catholic World*, November
Koch, T. W.	FIRST WORLD LIBRARY CONGRESS; BIBLIOGRAPHICAL EXHIBITS. *Library Journal*, October 1.
Millar, E. G.	THIRTEENTH CENTURY PORTABLE BIBLES. *International Studio*, August
Newton, A. E.	THIS BUSINESS OF BOOKS. *World's Work*, January
Rose, D.	THIS BOOK-COLLECTING GAME. *North American*, February
Rollins, C. P.	COMPLEAT COLLECTOR. *Saturday Review of Literature*, weekly numbers
Rollins, C. P.	FIFTY BOOKS; OR GOOD OR BAD; GROLIER CLUB EXHIBITIONS, 1929. *Saturday Review of Literature*, May 18.
Troxell, G. M.	JEROME KERN SALE. *Saturday Review of Literature*, January 12.
Troxell, G. M.	FASHION OF COLLECTING. *Saturday Review of Literature*, January 5.
Troxell, G. M.	JOHN CAMP WILLIAMS LIBRARY. *Saturday Review of Literature*, November 16.
Van Doren, Dorothy	SPECULATION IN BOOKS. *Nation*, February 6.
Wilcox, C. W.	FIRSTS THAT LAST. *Scribner's*, November
Winterich, J. T.	PRINTED AT AUTHOR'S EXPENSE. *Mentor*, January
Anonymous	UNCLE SAM COLLECTS RARE BIBLES. *Mentor*, June
Anonymous	BOOK COLLECTING FOR PROFIT. *Literary Digest*
Anonymous	COLLECTOR. *Canadian Bookman*, Monthly numbers from January, 1929

BOOKS ABOUT BOOKS

Anonymous	AMERICAN FIRST EDITIONS. *Publishers' Weekly*
Anonymous	RARE BOOKS AT WHOLESALE. *Publishers' Weekly*, November 16.
Anonymous	SPECULATION IN BOOKS. *Nation*, February 6.
Anonymous	BOOK GAMBLING GAME. *World's Work*, March

1930

Bennett, W.	REBUTTAL ON THE BROKEN TYPE THEORY; REJOINDER TO M. K. DUTTON. *Publishers' Weekly*, April 19.
Bliss, L. E.	HUNTINGTON LIBRARY. *Publishers' Weekly*, April 19.
Bowker, R. R.	VOLLBEHR PROFFER AND THE GUTENBERG BIBLE. *Library Journal*, March 1.
Carter, J.	ORIGINAL CONDITION. *Publishers' Weekly*, November 15.
Claudy, C.	GUTENBERG BIBLE FOR $8000! *Publishers' Weekly*, July 19.
Cohn, L. H.	BOOK MADNESS. *Scribner's*, May
Cornyn, J. H.	FINDING A LOST LITERATURE. *Pan-American Magazine*, August
Dutton, M. K.	IS THERE A FIRST IMPRESSION, REPLY TO W. BENNETT. *Publishers' Weekly*, March 15.
Ellsworth, E., Jr.	VOLUME ONE, NUMBER ONE. *Bookman*, December
Hamor, W. A., and Bass, L. W.	BIBLIOCHRESIS, THE PILOT OF RESEARCH. *Science*, April 11.
Hackett, E. B.	AMERICAN RARE BOOK TRADE SHOULD ORGANIZE; *Publishers' Weekly*, May 17.
Hopkins, F. M.	COLUMBIA UNIVERSITY ACQUIRES SELIGMAN COLLECTION OF WORKS ON ECONOMICS. *Publishers' Weekly*, April 5.
Hopkins, F. M.	ADVENTURES IN BOOK HUNTING. *Publishers' Weekly*, November 15.
Hopkins, F. M.	SALE OF THE LEHMANN LIBRARY. *Publishers' Weekly*, December 20.
Hopkins, F. M.	SERIOUS PROBLEM OF TODAY. *Publishers' Weekly*, November 15.
Hopkins, F. M.	TENDENCY OF AUCTION PRICES. *Publishers' Weekly*, November 15.
Hopkins, F. M.	SALE OF MODERN FIRST EDITIONS FROM THE LIBRARY OF A CHICAGO COLLECTOR BRINGS GOOD PRICES. *Publishers' Weekly*, March 15.

MAGAZINE REFERENCES

Hopkins, F. M.	SALE OF ILLUSTRATED BOOKS; CRINKSHANK COLLECTION AND COLORED PLATE BOOKS FROM THE GOLDSMITH-STERN SALOMONS LIBRARY. *Publishers' Weekly*, February 15.
Johnston, P.	FINE BOOKS IN THE PRESENT MARKET. *Publishers' Weekly*, September 6.
Kirsch, M. M.	BIBLIOGRAPHY INDISPENSABLE AID TO SOCIOLOGICAL RESEARCH. *Library Journal*, October 1.
LeCron, H. C	SOME RARE BOOKS YOU MAY HAVE MISSED. *Better Homes and Gardens*, November
Lloyd, R. B.	WHEN BOOKS WERE YOUNG; BOOK TRADE IN THE TWELFTH AND THIRTEENTH CENTURIES. *Fortnightly Review*, January
McKay, G. L.	EXHIBITION OF BOOKS AND MANUSCRIPTS ILLUSTRATING THE FORMATION OF THE ENGLISH LANGUAGE. *Publishers' Weekly*, April 19.
Merrill, M. C.	WHAT IS THE BEST SYSTEM OF PRESENTING BIBLIOGRAPHIES? *Science*, January 10.
St. John, J. L.	MORE ABOUT A UNIFORM BIBLIOGRAPHIC SYSTEM; REPLY TO M. C. MERRILL. *Science*, July 25.
Tester, A. C.	METHOD FOR MAKING A BIBLIOGRAPHY. *Science*, September 26.
Vincent, J. M.	BATTLE ABBEY RECORDS IN THE HUNTINGTON LIBRARY. *American History Review*, October
Weston, B. E.	SIXTY BOOKS IN FIVE INCHES. *Library Journal*, June 1.
Anonymous	BIBLE OF THE REVOLUTION; ROBERT AITKEN'S FIRST AMERICAN BIBLE TO BE PRINTED IN ENGLISH. *Publishers' Weekly*, November 15.
Anonymous	AMERICAN FIRST EDITIONS. *Publishers' Weekly*, August 16, October 18, December 20.
Anonymous	OUR BIBLE IN SPITE OF THE DEVIL; GUTENBERG BIBLE IN THE CONGRESSIONAL LIBRARY. *Literary Digest*, October 18.
Anonymous	TRAVELS OF THE T. C. COPY OF THE GUTENBERG BIBLE. *Libraries*, December

1931

Ashley, F. W.	GREATEST BOOK IN THE WORLD; GUTENBERG BIBLE. *School Life*, November

BOOKS ABOUT BOOKS

Bennett, W.	REMARKABLE FIRST EDITION OF HOYLE. *Publishers' Weekly*, July 18.
Briggs, M. H.	WESTERN AMERICAN REPLY TO A MENDOZA. *Publishers' Weekly*, March 7.
Carter, J.	LOOKING BACKWARD. *Publishers' Weekly*, January 19.
Carter, J.	LOOKING FORWARD. *Publishers' Weekly*, June 20.
Curtis, A. E.	VALUABLE OLD BOOKS. *Library Journal*, April 15.
Dawson, E.	RARE BOOK TRADE. *Publishers' Weekly*, April 18.
Dickerman, V.	COLLECTORS PRIZE RARE GOVERNMENT PUBLICATIONS. *School Life*, September
Harter, E.	LITTLE SIXTEENMO, THE GOOD COMPANION; HISTORY OF THE POCKET-SIZE BOOK FROM ALDUS MANUTIUS TO THE MODERN LIBRARY. *Publishers' Weekly*, October 10.
Hopkins, F. M.	RARE BOOK NOTES; ARREST OF DR. CLARKE IN BOSTON. *Publishers' Weekly*, June 20.
Hopkins, F. M.	JACKSON'S ANATOMY OF BIBLIOMANIA. *Publishers' Weekly*, January 7.
Hopkins, F. M.	COLLECTOR AND DEALER. *Publishers' Weekly*, November 1.
Hopkins, F. M.	RARE BOOK NOTES; OLIVE BRANCH PETITION OF THE SECOND CONTINENTAL CONGRESS TO GEORGE III. *Publishers' Weekly*, December 19.
Hopkins, F. M.	FIRST EDITIONS OF AMERICAN AUTHORS. *Publishers' Weekly*, November 21.
Hopkins, F. M.	APPRAISAL OF RARE BOOKS. *Publishers' Weekly*, November 21.
Hopkins, F. M.	OLD AND RARE BOOKS; MANUSCRIPTS OF THE MAYA PEOPLE BELIEVED TO HAVE BEEN MADE DECIPHERABLE BY DR. WILLIAM GATES. *Publishers' Weekly*, September 12.
Hopkins, F. M.	SUPREME EXHIBITION; ROSENBACH EXHIBITION OF AUTOGRAPHIC MATERIAL RELATING TO THE HISTORY OF AMERICA. *Publishers' Weekly*, April 18.
Hopkins, F. M.	QUERIES AND REPLIES. *Publishers' Weekly*, March 21.
Hopkins, F. M.	SALE OF LOTHIAN LIBRARY. *Publishers' Weekly*, November 21.
Hopkins, F. M.	AUCTION SALE AT PUTNAM'S. *Publishers' Weekly*, November 7.
Johnson, M.	FIRST EDITION NOTES. *Publishers' Weekly*, November 21.

MAGAZINE REFERENCES

Kopp, C. B.	GREAT AMERICAN LIBRARIES. *National Republic*, June
Lord, K.	BUDDING COLLECTORS. *Publishers' Weekly*, August 29.
Malvern, A. S.	TOMORROW'S RARITIES. *Saturday Evening Post*, January 10.
McFee, W.	PREFACE TO A BIBLIOGRAPHY. *Saturday Review of Literature*, October 3.
Mendoza, A.	SOME FIRSTS OF AMERICAN HUMOR, 1830-1875. *Publishers' Weekly*, March 21, April 18.
Mendoza, A.	BROADENING FIELD OF FIRSTS. *Publishers' Weekly*, January 17.
Newton, A. E.	BOOKS OF ONES OWN. *Atlantic Monthly*, October
Partington, W.	ABOUT BOOK-COLLECTING. *Bookman*, Monthly numbers from March
Putnam, H.	TREASURES IN THE NATIONAL LIBRARY. *Current History*, May
Rosenbach, A. S. W.	OLD MYSTERY BOOKS. *Saturday Evening Post*, September 5.
Rosenbach, A. S. W.	PRESIDENTS OF THE UNITED STATES AS BOOK COLLECTORS. *Libraries*, May
Trimble, N.	FUTURE OF FIRSTS. *Publishers' Weekly*, February 21.
Wells, G.	ANTIQUARIAN BOOKSELLER. *Saturday Review of Literature*, April 18.
Winterich, J. T.	EARLY AMERICAN BOOKS AND PRINTING. *Publishers' Weekly*, September 19, October 17, November 21, December 19.
Anonymous	AMERICAN FIRST EDITIONS. *Publishers' Weekly*, January 17, February 21, March 21, April 18, June 20, July 18, August 15, October 24, November 21, December 19.
Anonymous	COLLECTING AMERICAN LITERATURE. *Publishers' Weekly*, April 11.
Anonymous	PUBLIC LIBRARIES AND RARE BOOKS. *Libraries*, April
Anonymous	FIRST BOOK PRINTED IN BRAZIL. *Bulletin Pan-American Union*, May
Anonymous	EARLY PRINTED BOOKS; LOOE BABER COLLECTION. *Libraries*, July
Anonymous	COLLECTOR EXHIBITION OF FIRST EDITIONS OF THE FIRST BOOKS OF CANADIAN WRITERS. *Canadian Bookman*, July
Anonymous	THEFT OF RARE BOOKS. *Libraries*, March

BOOKS ABOUT BOOKS

Anonymous — RARE BOOK THIEF CAUGHT. *Publishers' Weekly*, June 13.

1932

Becker, M. L. — READER'S GUIDE; MAGAZINES ON BOOK COLLECTING. *Saturday Review of Literature*, May 28

Borden, A. K. — STUDY OF BIBLIOGRAPHY. *School and Society*, February 13.

Brooke, W. R. — SHOESTRING BOOK-COLLECTOR. *Bookman*, March

Buxbaum, E. C. — ADVENTURES IN BOOKS WANTED. *Publishers' Weekly*, September 24.

Carter, J. — BIBLIOGRAPHY AND THE COLLECTOR. *Publishers' Weekly*, November 19.

Cunningham, H. F. — DRY BOOK COLLECTING. *Bookman*, September

Hartley, H. H. — RARE BOOKS IN THE COAST AND GEODETIC SURVEY LIBRARY. *Scientific Monthly*, August

Hopkins, F. M. — OLD AND RARE BOOKS; FIVE CENTURIES OF BOOK MAKING, ROSENBACH COMPANY'S GALLERIES, PHILADELPHIA. *Publishers' Weekly*, January 9.

Hopkins, F. M. — STARTING THE BOOK COLLECTOR. *Publishers' Weekly*, November 19.

Marks, F. X. — HUMANIZING YOUR STOCK OF LIMITED AND SPECIAL EDITIONS. *Publishers' Weekly*, November 5.

Manks, D. S. — BIBLIOGRAPHY, AN URGENT PART OF WORKS. *Library Journal*, September 1.

Rosenbach, A. S. W. — TRAIL OF SCARLET. *Saturday Evening Post*, October 1.

Shaw, R. K. — PERFECT BIBLIOMANIAC. *Library Journal*, December 15.

Stonehill, C. A., Jr. — ON BOOKSELLERS. *Saturday Review of Literature*, May 14.

Winterich, J. T. — EARLY AMERICAN BOOKS AND PRINTING. *Publishers' Weekly*, January 16, February 20, March 19, May 21.

Winterich, J. T. — LOTHIAN SALE WITH SUMMARY OF THE LOTS AND THE PRICES REALIZED. *Saturday Review of Literature*, February 6.

Anonymous — BOOKS ARE DOOMED. *Saturday Review of Literature*, January 16.

Anonymous — COLLECTOR. *Canadian Bookman*, January and February

Anonymous — AMERICAN FIRST EDITIONS. *Publishers' Weekly*, January 16, February 20, April 16, May 21, June 18, July 16, August 20.

MAGAZINE REFERENCES

Anonymous	SCHOLARLY SIDE OF THE RARE BOOK BUSINESS. *Publishers' Weekly*, November 19.
Anonymous	BOOK THEFTS. *Publishers' Weekly*, September 17.
Anonymous	WHO WILL BE WORTHY IN A HUNDRED YEARS? *Literary Digest*, October 1.

1933

Cannon, C.	OUT-OF-PRINT BOOK LISTS; RETURNS ON QUESTIONNAIRE. *Library Journal*, June 1.
Cleaveland, M.	MISSING BOOKS AGAIN! *Wilson Bulletin*, April
Currier, I. R. A.	RECKLESS RALPH STILL PURSUES 'EM; COLLECTOR OF PENNY DREADFULS. *American Magazine*, February
Dickson, L. M.	OLD BOOKS. *Canadian Bookman*, March
Farndale, W. G.	BOOKS OF ONE'S OWN. *Library Journal*, June 1.
Hopkins, F. M.	OLD RARE BOOKS; AMERICANA FROM THE LIBRARY OF THE LATE LEVI Z. LEITER. *Publishers' Weekly*, March 11.
Hopkins, F. M.	SALE OF VICKERY LIBRARY. *Publishers' Weekly*, March 18.
Hopkins, F. M.	RARE BOOK NOTES. *Publishers' Weekly*, July 1932 to June 1933.
Hopkins, F. M.	TRENDS IN BOOK COLLECTING. *Publishers' Weekly*, November 18.
Hopkins, F. M.	INTERVIEW WITH A LEADER OF THE RARE BOOK TRADE. *Publishers' Weekly*, November 18.
Hopkins, F. M.	STANDARDIZING CATALOGUING TERMS. *Publishers' Weekly*, November 18.
Hopkins, F. M.	RARE BOOK NOTES. *Publishers' Weekly*, third number of each month.
Hopkins, F. M.	OLD AND RARE BOOKS. *Publishers' Weekly*, weekly numbers.
Hopkins, F. M.	AUCTION SEASON OF 1932-33. *Publishers' Weekly*, November 18.
Iiams, I. M.	PRESERVATION OF RARE BOOKS AND MANUSCRIPTS. *Saturday Review of Literature*, September 7.
Johnson, P.	ENCOURAGE COLLECTING. *Publishers' Weekly*, September 23.
Kyte, E. C.	FROM THE BINDING. *Queen's Quarterly*, February
Partington, W.	ABOUT BOOK-COLLECTING. *Bookman*, Monthly numbers

BOOKS ABOUT BOOKS

Radoff, M. L.	CENSORSHIP AMONG THE LEARNED. *American Mercury*, February
Rollins, C. P. and Winterich, J. T.	COMPLEAT COLLECTOR. *Saturday Review of Literature*, Numbers from July 1932 to June 1933.
Rosenbach, A. S. W.	EARLY AMERICAN CHILDREN'S BOOKS. *Publishers' Weekly*, May 20.
Symons, A. J. A.	MODERN FIRST EDITION MARKET. *Fortnightly*, April
Winterich, J. T.	GOOD SECOND-HAND CONDITION. *Publishers' Weekly*, third number of each month, July 1932-July 1933.
Anonymous	RAREST OF LINCOLNIANA; ROSENBACH COLLECTION. *Publishers' Weekly*, February 18.
Anonymous	AMERICAN FIRST EDITIONS. *Publishers' Weekly*, August 19, September 16.

1934

Barnett, L. K.	NIMROD ON A BOOKSHELF; A. B. MACLAY COLLECTION. *Country Life*, February.
Bates, G.	STANDARDIZING CATALOG TERMS. *Publishers' Weekly*, May 19.
Birss, J. H.	AMERICAN FIRST EDITIONS (of A. Edward Newton). *Publishers' Weekly*, November 3.
Brewer, R. A.	HUNTING TREASURES IN RARE BOOKS. *Popular Mechanics*, July
Brown, K.	IN THE FIELD OF BIBLIOGRAPHY. *Library Journal*, March 15.
Devoe, A.	BOOKS BY THE ROADSIDE. *Atlantic Monthly*, January
Grubbe, G. H.	LOOK UP YOUR FIRST EDITIONS. *Canadian Bookman*, January
Hopkins, F. M.	BOOKBINDERS' PLIGHT; SHOULD FIRST EDITIONS BE REBOUND? *Publishers' Weekly*, February 17.
Hopkins, F. M.	RARITIES BRING GOOD PRICES. *Publishers' Weekly*, April 21.
Hopkins, F. M.	SALE OF TERRY LIBRARY. *Publishers' Weekly*, May 19.
Hopkins, F. M.	PART TWO OF TERRY LIBRARY. *Publishers' Weekly*, November 17.
Hopkins, F. M.	RARE BOOK TRADE RECOVERY. *Publishers' Weekly*, July 21.
Hopkins, F. M.	RULES OF THE CHASE. *Publishers' Weekly*, November 17.

MAGAZINE REFERENCES

Hopkins, F. M.	AUCTION SEASON OF 1933-34 AND PROSPECTS OF THE NEW SEASON. *Publishers' Weekly*, November 17.
Hopkins, F. M.	OLD AND RARE BOOKS. *Publishers' Weekly*, weekly numbers
Randall, D. A.	BIBLIOGRAPHICAL SENSATION, another review of the Carter Pollard book. *Publishers' Weekly*, July 7.
Rollins, C. P. and J. T. Winterich	COMPLETE COLLECTOR. *Saturday Review of Literature*, various numbers.
Tinker, C. B.	BIBLIOGRAPHICAL HOAX, Review of an Enquiry into the Nature of Certain 19th Century Pamphlets, by J. Carter and G. Pollard. *Publishers' Weekly*, July 7.
Winterich, J. T.	LIBRARIES AS COLLECTORS. *Saturday Review of Literature*, September 8.
Winterich, J. T.	WHO SAYS THERE'S NOTHING LEFT TO COLLECT? *Publishers' Weekly*, November 17.
Anonymous	VALUABLE COLLECTORS ITEMS DECLARED TO BE FORGERIES. *Literary Digest*, June 23.
Anonymous	CUSTOMS BUREAU SEES THE LIGHT: NEW RULING CONCERNING RARE BOOKS. *Publishers' Weekly*, November 10.
Anonymous	AMERICAN FIRST EDITIONS. *Publishers' Weekly*, January 20, March 17.
Anonymous	SOME 19th CENTURY RARITIES MAY BE EXTREMELY CLEVER FORGERIES. *Publishers' Weekly*, June 2.

1935

Bates, G.	CHILDREN'S CORNER: TRIBUTE TO THE FIRST REAL CHILDREN'S BOOK PUBLISHED. *Publishers' Weekly*, October 26.
Bennett, C. A.	BOOK THAT HAS OUTLIVED ITS GENERATION: BRITISH CARPENTER BY F. PRICE, PRINTED IN 1735. *Industrial Education Magazine*, September
Bendikson, L.	SOME PHOTOTECHNICAL METHODS FOR THE PRESERVATION AND RESTORATION OF THE CONTENTS OF DOCUMENTS. *Library Journal*, October 1.
Benet, W. R.	PHOENIXIANA; OR, SKETCHES AND BURLESQUES BY YOURS RESPECTIVELY, JOHN B. SQUIBOB. *Saturday Review of Literature*, July 20.

BOOKS ABOUT BOOKS

Devoe, A.	THRILL OF BOOK COLLECTING. *Rotarian*, January
Hall, H.	NEW PILGRIMAGE TO SAN MARINO; ENGLISH LOCAL RECORDS IN CALIFORNIA. *Contemporary Age*, August
Hopkins, F. M.	AUCTION SEASON OF 1934-35 AND PROSPECTS OF THE PRESENT SEASON. *Publishers' Weekly*, October 26.
Hopkins, F. M.	LAST MONTH'S BOOK SALES. *Publishers' Weekly*, January 19, February 16, March 16, April 20, November 23 and December 21.
Hopkins, F. M.	LONDON AUCTION SEASON. *Publishers' Weekly*, September 21.
Hopkins, F. M.	MATHER LIBRARY SOLD TO T. W. MAC GREGOR. *Publishers' Weekly*, December 21.
Hopkins, F. M.	OGDEN GOELET COLLECTION. *Publishers' Weekly*, January 19.
Hopkins, F. M.	OLD AND RARE BOOKS. *Publishers' Weekly*
Hopkins, F. M.	PRICES CONTINUE TO ADVANCE. *Publishers' Weekly*, December 21.
Hopkins, F. M.	RARE BOOK NOTES; EXHIBITION OF MANUSCRIPTS AND PRINTED BOOKS, ILLUSTRATING DEVELOPMENT OF AMERICAN AND ENGLISH LAW. *Publishers' Weekly*, August 17.
Hopkins, F. M.	RARITIES BRING GOOD PRICES AT FIRST IMPORTANT SALE OF SEASON. *Publishers' Weekly*, November 23.
Hopkins, F. M.	SALES SEASON CLOSES. *Publishers' Weekly*, June 15.
Hopkins, F. M.	VALUABLE COLLECTIONS SOLD: STETSON LIBRARY AND SELECTIONS OF FIRST EDITIONS, AUTOGRAPH LETTERS AND MANUSCRIPTS, ASSOCIATION BOOKS AND OTHER ITEMS OF OUTSTANDING IMPORTANCE. *Publishers' Weekly*, May 18.
Hopkins, F. M.	LAST MONTH'S BOOK SALES. *Publishers' Weekly*, Jan. 19, Feb. 16, March 16, April 20, Nov. 23, Dec. 21.
Leete, W.	NOT OF AN AGE, BUT FOR ALL TIME; SHAKESPEARE FOLIOS AT AUCTION. *Theatre Arts Monthly*, January
McNeil, P. A.	RARE BOOKS IN THE OLIVEIRA LIMA LIBRARY. *Bulletin of Pan-American Union*, June
Morley, Christopher	LETTERS TO HINNULEO. *Saturday Review of Literature*, April 6.
Morley, Christopher	REASONS OF MY OWN. *Saturday Review of Literature*, April 13.

MAGAZINE REFERENCES

Rosenbach, A. S. W.	OLD ALMANACS AND PROGNOSTICATIONS. *Saturday Evening Post*, June 8.
Winterich, J. T.	COMPLEAT COLLECTOR. *Saturday Review of Literature*, alternate numbers
Winterich, J. T.	HUNTINGTONANA. *Saturday Review of Literature*, May 11.
Anonymous	AMERICAN FIRST EDITIONS. *Publishers' Weekly*, Jan. 19, March 16, April 20, May 18, June 15, July 20, Nov. 23.

1936

Armstrong, E. V.	PLAYGROUND OF A SCIENTIST; EDGAR F. SMITH COLLECTION IN THE HISTORY OF CHEMISTRY. *Scientific Monthly*, April
Birks, G. F.	HOBBYHORSE HITCHING POST. *Rotarian*, December
Blanck, J. (ed.)	AMERICAN BOOK-PRICES CURRENT; REPORTS FROM AUCTION SALES. *Publishers' Weekly*, November 7, December 5, 19.
Blanck, J.	NEWS FROM THE RARE BOOK SHOPS. *Publishers' Weekly*, November 28, December 12-26.
Blanck, J. (ed.)	LIBRARY OF ARTHUR MACHEMER, WITH ADDITIONS. *Publishers' Weekly*, November 28.
Bockwitz, H. H.	BOOKS, IN SPITE OF FIRE AND SWORD; EUROPE'S ZEAL FOR PRESERVING THE WRITTEN RECORDS OF MAN'S THINKING. *Rotarian*, December
Budd, R.	WRENN COLLECTION OF RARE BOOKS. *The Library Journal*, February 15.
Burgess, A. P.	FURTHER EXCAVATING. *The Library Journal*, April 15.
Devoe, A.	BOOKS UNSUNG, *Scribner's Magazine*, April
Dodge, N. L.	RARE BOOK HUNTER'S PRAYER. *Publishers' Weekly*, June 6.
Hare, J.	BIOGRAPHY OF A BOOK COLLECTOR; POEM. *The Library Journal*, March
Hopkins, F. M.	AMERICAN BOOK PRICES CURRENT 1935. *Publishers' Weekly*, January 18.
Hopkins, F. M.	AMERICAN FIRST EDITIONS; BEGINNING OF COLLECTING FIFTY YEARS AGO AND THE GREAT ADVANCE IN PRICES SINCE. *Publishers' Weekly*, August 15.
Hopkins, F. M.	AUCTION BIDS BY MAIL. *Publishers' Weekly*, February 15.
Hopkins, F. M.	AUCTION SEASON OF 1935-36 AND PROSPECTS OF THE PRESENT SEASON. *Publishers' Weekly*, November 28.

BOOKS ABOUT BOOKS

Hopkins, F. M.	BOOK SALES BEFORE THE HOLIDAYS. *Publishers' Weekly*, December 19.
Hopkins, F. M.	FIRST SALE OF THE NEW YEAR. *Publishers' Weekly*, January 18.
Hopkins, F. M.	LAST MONTH'S BOOK SALES. *Publishers' Weekly*, February 15, March 21, April 18, May 16.
Hopkins, F. M.	LIBRARY OF JUSTICE O. W. HOLMES BEQUEATHED TO THE LIBRARY OF CONGRESS. *Publishers' Weekly*, February 1.
Hopkins, F. M.	MAINZ CATHOLICON OF 1460. *Publishers' Weekly*, November 28.
Hopkins, F. M.	OLD AND RARE BOOKS. *Publishers' Weekly*
Hopkins, F. M.	OLD AND RARE BOOKS; M. J. PERRY LIBRARY. *Publishers' Weekly*, February 29.
Hopkins, F. M.	ONE MILLION VISITORS. *Publishers' Weekly*, January 25.
Hopkins, F. M.	RARE BOOK NOTES. *Publishers' Weekly*, third number of each month
Hopkins, F. M.	RARE BOOK NOTES; SALE OF THE NEWTON PAPERS. *Publishers' Weekly*, July 25, August 15.
Johnson, E. D.	EXCAVATING IN A LIBRARY; CONTENT OF THE PRIVATE LIBRARY OF THE EIGHTEENTH CENTURY SOUTH. *The Library Journal*, March 1.
Lehmann-Haupt, H.	BOOKS ABOUT BOOKMAKING. *Publishers' Weekly*, January 4, March 7, April 4, May 2, June 6, August 1, September 5, November 7.
Lloyd, J. H.	REPRODUCTIONS FROM GEORGE WASHINGTON'S COPYBOOK. *School Life*, February
Osborne, L. E.	EXHIBITION OF RARE BOOKS GIVEN BY THE HON. ALFRED C. CHAPIN TO WILLIAMS COLLEGE. *The Library Journal*, May 15.
Randall, D. A.	KIPLING AND COLLECTING. *Publishers' Weekly*, January 25.
Rosenbach, A. S. W.	MIGHTY WOMEN BOOK HUNTERS. *Publishers' Weekly*, October 10.
Weston, B. E.	MCGREGOR COLLEGE PLAN TO AID COLLEGE LIBRARIES IN THE COLLECTION AND PRESERVATION OF RARE AMERICANA. *The Library Journal*, November 15.
Winterich, J. T.	COMPARATIVE LITERATURE. *Saturday Review of Literature*, March 14.

MAGAZINE REFERENCES

Winterich, J. T.	LEARY'S CENTENARY 1836-1936. *Publishers' Weekly*, June 6.
Winterich, J. T.	MAN BEHIND THE BOOK. *Publishers' Weekly*, November 28.
Zoeller, K. W.	JEWELL FOR GENTRIE; NEW YORK PUBLIC LIBRARY EXHIBIT OF SPORTING BOOKS. *Country Life*, October
Anonymous	AMERICAN FIRST EDITIONS. *Publishers' Weekly*, February 15, March 21, April 19, June 20, August 22, November 28, December 19.
Anonymous	COLLECTOR. *Canadian Bookman*, December 5-7.
Anonymous	READERS; MCGUFFEY'S EDIFYING TEXTS BECOME MUSEUM PIECES. *News Week*, July 25.
Anonymous	WHEN MONEY'S NO OBJECT. *Publishers' Weekly*, September 12.

1937

Blanck, J. (ed.)	AMERICAN BOOK-PRICES CURRENT; REPORTS FROM AUCTION SALES. *Publishers' Weekly*, January 2, 16-March 13, 27-May 15, 29.
Blanck, J.	NEWS FROM THE RARE BOOK SHOPS. *Publishers' Weekly*, January 9-February 6, 20-27, March 13-27, April 10-24, May 8, 29.
Devoe, A.	ADVENTURES OF A BOOKMAN. *American Mercury*, February
Fuller, R. F.	BOOKSELLER COUNTS HIS BOOKS. *Atlantic Monthly*, January; *Publishers' Weekly*, January 9.
Hopkins, F. M.	AMERICAN BOOK-PRICES CURRENT, 1936. Review; *Publishers' Weekly*, February 20.
Hopkins, F. M.	FIRST SALE OF THE NEW YEAR. *Publishers' Weekly*, January 16.
Hopkins, F. M.	GLANCE BACKWARD AND FORWARD. *Publishers' Weekly*, March 20.
Hopkins, F. M.	LAST MONTH'S BOOK SALES. *Publishers' Weekly*, May 15.
Lehmann-Haupt, H.	BOOKS ABOUT BOOKMAKING. *Publishers' Weekly*, January 2, March 6, May 1.
Melcher, F. G.	BOOK PRICES AND THE PUBLIC. *Atlantic Monthly*, March
Melcher, F. G.	PRICE OF A BOOK. *Publishers' Weekly*, April 10.
Morley, C.	NEW BODLEIAN. *Saturday Review of Literature*, March 13.

BOOKS ABOUT BOOKS

Smith, J. F.	BOOKPLATES COLLECTION; LIVERPOOL PUBLIC LIBRARIES, ENGLAND. *The Library Journal*, March 15.
Weston, B. E.	NEW BOOKPLATE FOR RARE BOOK COLLECTION, LIBRARY OF CONGRESS. *The Library Journal*, May 1.
Weston, B. E.	SURVEY OF SPECIAL COLLECTIONS IN NEW JERSEY. *The Library Journal*, January 15.
Willoughby, E. E.	CATALOGING THE EARLY PRINTED ENGLISH BOOKS OF THE FOLGER SHAKESPEARE LIBRARY. *The Library Journal*, April 15.
Wilson, M.	GAME IS IN THE PLAYING; BOOKS COSTING NOT MORE THAN FIFTEEN CENTS. *The Library Journal*, June 1.
Anonymous	AMERICAN FIRST EDITIONS. *Publishers' Weekly*, March 20, April 17, May 15.
Anonymous	COLLECTOR. *Canadian Bookman*, March 9-10.
Anonymous	FACSIMILES OF FAMOUS BIBLE OF BORSO D'ESTE. *Christian Science Monitor Weekly Magazine Section*, April 21.
Anonymous	TO SATISFY HIS FANCY. *Publishers' Weekly*, May 22.

CHAPTER IV

Glossary

1. Americana	Books relating not only to the United States but also to North, South and Central America.
2. Antiquary	A student of old times through relics, one who collects or studies antiquities, of which old books may be an example.
3. Antique Paper	That which is not finished by machine and which retains its natural rough state.
4. Antiquart	German for "second-hand book shop."
5. Association Books	Those inscribed by author or previously owned by or presented to a prominent person.
6. Bibelot	A book of very small size.
7. Biblio	Signifying or pertaining to books.
8. Bibliographer	One who describes and writes about books. The author of a bibliography.
9. Bibliography	The technical description and classification of books, or a list of any author's books or a list of books pertaining to the same subject.
10. Bibliolatry	The extravagant admiration of books.
11. Bibliokleptomaniac	An insane book thief.
12. Bibliomaniac	Quite literally, one who is crazy about books. Most book collectors appreciate this descriptive phrase at their expense, for, in its way, it is a compliment. The collector who hears himself referred to in this fashion may consider that he has "arrived."
13. Bibliophile	A true lover of books who collects and reads for his own pleasure without consideration of what others may think of his tastes.
14. Bibliopole	Bookseller.

BOOKS ABOUT BOOKS

15. Bibliotaphe	The collector who is afraid of loss and keeps his books locked up.
16. Bibliopolist	A dealer in second-hand books.
17. Black-letter	The name given in English to the character of the type which succeeded the Gothic.
18. Block-books	Books printed from engraved blocks of wood in Holland, Flanders and Germany during the fifteenth century.
19. Boards	A book is said to be bound in boards when the back is covered with paper or cloth.
20. Book of Hours or Horae	A book containing prayers for laymen. Books of this kind are numbered among the most beautiful ever produced just prior to and after the invention of printing.
21. Bowdlerized	An expurgated book, the term originating from Thomas Bowdler who published an altered edition of Shakespeare in 1818.
22. Broadside or Broadsheet	Printing on one side only.
23. Brochure	A publication or pamphlet limited in extent.
24. Buckram	Heavy cloth binding with a light coat of color.
25. Cancels	Pages containing errors which are to be cut out and replaced by others properly printed which are generally supplied with the last sheet.
26. Catalogue Raisonné	A systematic list of books arranged according to subjects.
27. Chapbook	A small cheap book with paper binding published in England and the American Colonies in the seventeenth and eighteenth centuries.
28. Circa	Latin prepostion for an approximate date.
29. Cloth Boards	A stiff binding covered with cloth.
30. Codex	A manuscript book of the Scriptures or classics written upon vellum tablets or rolls of papyrus.
31. Collate	To examine and compare point by point a questionable book with a known true copy.
32. Colophon	Webster says, "The conclusion of a book containing the place or year, or both, of its publication."
33. Contemporary Binding	One made within the period of publication of the book.

GLOSSARY

34.	Cuneiform writing	Characters of wedge shape, originating some 6000 years ago and used until the third century B.C. by the Assyrians and Babylonians.
35.	DeLuxe	Finely printed books upon a good quality of paper and limited in number.
36.	Desiderata	A list of books wanted.
37.	Duodecimo	Twelvemo or 12mo. The size of a book printed on paper folded into twelve leaves or twenty-four pages. The signatures are B, B2, B3, on the first, third and ninth pages. The wire mark is horizontal and the paper mark on the fore-edge. The usual sizes are 12mo and royal or long 12mo.
38.	Edito Princeps	Similar in meaning to First Edition.
39.	End-papers	The leaves containing no printing at the beginning and end of a book.
40.	Ex Libris	Latin for "from the books," a widely used bookplate phrase.
41.	Extra Illustrated	The mounting and inlaying of extra material or engravings to a bound volume or set of books.
42.	Folio	The size of a book printed on paper of whatever dimensions which, when folded into two leaves, makes four pages. A folio sheet may be known by the watermarks, these being always perpendicular with the paper mark in the center.
43.	Fore-edge	The front edge of a book which, when decorated, becomes known as fore-edge printing or painting.
44.	Format	A general term pertaining to the size, binding, type and general make-up or construction of a book.
45.	Foxed	Stained or mouldy leaves.
46.	Grolier	The term used in describing a particular kind of ornamental leather binding originated by a Frenchman, Jean Grolier (1479-1565), whose great collection of books were beautifully bound in a distinctive style which is still imitated.
47.	Half-bound	When the sides of a book are covered with paper or cloth and the corners and back are leather bound.
48.	Half-title	When the full title of a book is preceded by a sub-title.
49.	Impression	A number of copies printed at any one time.

BOOKS ABOUT BOOKS

50. Incunabula — The first printed books before 1501.
51. Large Paper Copies — Books printed on paper of extra size with wide margins. This form of printing was not in use except in one or two isolated instances until after 1600.
52. Levant Morocco — A large-grained heavy grade of morocco leather.
53. Marginalia — Notes on the margins of pages in a book.
54. Mint — Catalogue term for a book in immaculate condition as it came from the printer.
55. Morocco — Leather made from goatskin. One of the most durable bookbinding leathers.
56. Octavo (8vo) — The size of a book printed on paper of any dimensions which, when folded into eight leaves, makes sixteen pages. The signatures are B, B2, B3, on pages 1, 3, 5. The wire mark is vertical and the paper mark at the top is usually considerably cut in binding. The usual sizes are 8vo, royal 8vo, demy 8vo, crown 8vo, post 8vo, and foolscap 8vo.
57. Out of Print — A book may be said to be out of print when the publisher has no more copies for sale.
58. Pamphlet — Any printed work, the sheets of which are stitched together but which is unbound. It may or may not have a paper wrapper or cover.
59. Quarto (4to) — The size of a book printed on paper of any dimensions which, when folded into four leaves, makes eight pages. The signatures are B, B2, on pages 1 and 3. The water mark is always horizontal and the paper mark folded in half on the back of the book is still midway between the top and the bottom.
60. Rare — A book may be said to be rare when only a few copies, not easily met with, are in one's own country.

Very Rare—When the copies of a book are so dispersed that there are but few of them even in near-by countries and it is, therefore, increasingly difficult to get them.

Extremely Rare—Books limited to fifty or sixty scattered copies.

Excessively Rare—When there are not more than ten copies in the world.

GLOSSARY

61. Rubbed	A book is rubbed when the binding shows signs of wear.
62. Seventy-Twomo (72mo)	A sheet of paper folded into 72 leaves making 144 pages.
63. Ser-decimo (16mo)	The size of a book or paper folded into 16 leaves making 32 pages. The signatures are B, B2, B3, B4, B5, B6, B7, B8; on pages 1, 3, 5, 7, 9, 11, and 15. The wire mark is horizontal with the paper mark on the fore-edge.
64. Signatures	The capital letters or figures under the foot line of the first page of each sheet to indicate their order in binding. They originated either in Milan in 1470 or in Cologne in 1472, there being some difference of opinion among authorities. The first sheet of every book is usually begun with the signature B, leaving A for the title sheet.
65. Sixty-fourmo (64mo)	A sheet of paper folded into 64 leaves making 128 pages.
66. Solander	A book shaped box in which to keep or encase books in paper parts or any other material. Invented by Daniel C. Solander, a botanist, one time Keeper of Printed Books in the British Museum.
67. Sub-title	The half-title sometimes found before the main title of a book.
68. Tail-piece	An ornament placed on a short page to fill up a vacancy.
69. Tall Copy	A book that has lost no part of its height in binding.
70. Thirty-sixmo (36mo)	A sheet of paper folded into 36 leaves making 72 pages.
71. Thirty-twomo (32mo)	As above, folded into 32 leaves making 64 pages.
72. Tree Calf	A full calf binding stained with a tree-like design.
73. Twenty-fourmo (24mo)	The same, folded into 24 leaves making 48 pages.
74. Twentymo (20mo)	The same, folded into 20 leaves making 40 pages.
75. Uncut and Un-opened	Two of the most confusing terms used in describing books. A book is uncut when the top, fore-edge, or bottom of its pages has not been cut or pruned square by the knife of the binder. A book is un-

BOOKS ABOUT BOOKS

	opened when the pages have not been slit to permit of reading. A book may be opened by slitting the pages yet still remain uncut.
76. Verso	The pages of a book on the reverse or left-hand side. The opposite of recto. A verso page always carries the even number in pagination.
77. Wrapper	The paper cover of a book.

SOUTHEASTERN MASSACHUSETTS UNIVERSITY
Z1002.W37 1974
Books about books

3 2922 00184 252 2